SCHOLASTIC

The BIG BOOK of Reading Response Activities

by Michael Gravois

New York • Toronto • London • Auckland • Sydney
Mexico City • New Delhi • Hong Kong • Buenos Aires

Teaching
Resources

► Dedication

To Betty Hancock,
David and Gayle Lund,
Andy, Chrissie, and Mackenzie Lund,
and Julie Lund

It is not flesh and blood
but the heart that makes us family.

Cover design by Jason Robinson
Interior design by Michael Gravois
Illustrations by Mike Moran and Dave Clegg

ISBN–13: 978-0-439-76062-1
ISBN–10: 0-439-76062-3

Contents

Postreading Activities

Introduction

Creating a book-rich environment is the first step toward developing a literate classroom community where children learn to read and read to learn. Reading, the most essential of subjects, is the cornerstone to success in all other areas of study. However, children don't learn to read simply by being exposed to books. Reading must be taught. As an effective teacher you not only strengthen children's reading skills but help nurture a lifelong love of reading.

This book is designed to help you cultivate a classroom filled with enthusiastic readers by providing you with scores of hands-on activities, projects, bulletin boards, and creative dramatic ideas that are sure to get your students excited about reading, talking about reading, and writing about reading. These activities will encourage students to become active participants in their own learning. And an involved student is an engaged one.

Using This Book

This book is divided into three main sections—prereading activities, reading activities, and postreading activities (although a few of the activities span across all three phases of reading). Certainly, many of the activities can be shifted to another category or adapted to meet your needs. So look through the book and explore the possibilities.

Prereading activities prepare students for the thoughtful process involved in reading. Some of these activities are designed to teach students about the nature of reading and the parts of a book; others are meant to help develop important reading skills—such as prediction, learning new vocabulary, and identifying major story elements.

Reading activities develop students' awareness of essential practices that proficient readers possess—examining character relationships, comprehending the main idea of a passage, and connecting themes from a book to their own life experiences.

Postreading activities require students to reflect on the act of reading. They ask students to recall information from the readings, offer opinions about what they've read, and celebrate their reading accomplishments.

Teacher Tip

The activities in this book are categorized as prereading, reading, and postreading activities, but most can easily be adapted to fit any category. Most also work well with either fiction or nonfiction books, as independent or small-group projects, or as in-class or homework assignments. When selecting an activity, determine how it can best be used to meet the needs of your class.

Teacher Tip

Remember to consider your students' interests when planning your reading lessons and choosing the books you're going to use. Selecting books that appeal to students— both in content and in theme—can ensure that you will soon have a class of avid readers.

Teacher Tip

Spend time in your local and school libraries. Learn about the quality children's books that are available. Become an expert in the books at your students' various learning levels. Knowing which book to recommend to which student is one of the keys to being an outstanding teacher.

Book Talk

"Reading, in contrast to sitting before the screen, is not a purely passive exercise. The child, particularly one who reads a book dealing with real life, has nothing before it but the hieroglyphics of the printed page. Imagination must do the rest; and imagination is called upon to do it. Not so the television screen. Here everything is spelled out for the viewer, visually, in motion, and in all three dimensions. No effort of imagination is called upon for its enjoyment."
—George F. Kennan, "American Addictions," *New Oxford Review*, June 1993.

Check the header bar at the top of each activity's title page to determine the skill being covered and the type of activity it is. There are four major types of activities in this book:

- **Projects:** These are hands-on projects that ask students to create a manipulative of some sort or that encourage the students to interact with each other and discuss aspects of reading. Most of the projects are adaptable; you can use them with students working in groups, pairs, or as individuals.

- **Graphic Organizers:** These help students organize their thoughts as they respond to the act of reading. Templates are provided for you to copy and pass out to the class.

- **Bulletin Boards:** These activities help you create an environment that gives the students ownership of their space by surrounding them with examples of their own work.

- **Creative Dramatics:** In its simplest form, creative dramatics is structured play. Creative dramatics promotes social skills, literacy skills, confidence, independent thought, and problem-solving skills. And they are sure to fill your classroom with laughter.

The sidebars of this book offer tips and advice related to each activity:

- **Teacher Tip**—These tips suggest extensions and alternative uses for the activities.

- **Cross-Curriculum**—Learn ways in which the activities can be used in other subject areas.

- **Book Talk**—Read what the experts have to say about different reading skills and strategies.

The activities in this book are organized around a common theme—celebrating reading. They approach the topic from a variety of perspectives and are meant to help you tap into the individual strengths of students to help them form a bridge of knowledge between the books they read and their own lives.

But above all, use the ideas in this book to keep the school days interesting, challenging, and fun, and you'll soon find that you've created an environment in which literacy thrives.

Connections to the Language Arts Standards

The activities in this book help students meet the language arts standards outlined by Mid-continent Research for Education and Learning (www.mcrel.org), a nationally recognized nonprofit organization that collects and synthesizes national and state K–12 standards.

Uses the general skills and strategies of the writing process
- Uses a variety of strategies to plan research (e.g., identifies possible topic by brainstorming, listing questions, using idea webs; organizes prior knowledge about a topic; develops a course of action; determines how to locate necessary information)
- Writes in response to literature (e.g., summarizes main ideas and significant details; relates own ideas to supporting details; advances judgments; supports judgments with references to the text, other works, other authors, nonprint media, and personal knowledge)

Uses the general skills and strategies of the reading process
- Establishes a purpose for reading (e.g., for information, for pleasure, to understand a specific viewpoint)
- Makes, confirms, and revises simple predictions about what will be found in a text (e.g., uses prior knowledge and ideas presented in text, illustrations, titles, topic sentences, key words, and foreshadowing clues)

Uses reading skills and strategies to understand and interpret a variety of literary texts
- Uses reading skills and strategies to understand a variety of literary passages and texts (e.g., fairy tales, folktales, fiction, nonfiction, myths, poems, fables, fantasies, historical fiction, biographies, autobiographies, chapter books)
- Understands the basic concept of plot (e.g., main problem, conflict, resolution, cause and effect)
- Understands elements of character development in literary works (e.g., differences between main and minor characters; stereotypical characters as opposed to fully developed characters; changes that characters undergo; the importance of a character's actions, motives, and appearance to plot and theme)
- Makes connections between characters or simple events in a literary work and people or events in his or her own life

Uses reading skills and strategies to understand and interpret a variety of informational texts
- Understands the main idea and supporting details of simple expository information
- Uses the various parts of a book (e.g., index, table of contents, glossary, appendix, preface) to locate information
- Summarizes and paraphrases information in texts (e.g., includes the main idea and significant supporting details of a reading selection)

Uses listening and speaking strategies for different purposes
- Makes contributions in class and group discussions (e.g., reports on ideas and personal knowledge about a topic, initiates conversations, connects ideas and experiences with those of others)
- Recites and responds to familiar stories, poems, and rhymes with patterns (e.g., relates information to own life; describes character, setting, plot)
- Listens for specific information in spoken texts (e.g., plot details or information about a character in a short story read aloud, information about a familiar topic from a radio broadcast)

Kendall, J. S., & Marzano, R. J. (2004). *Content knowledge: A compendium of standards and benchmarks for K–12 education.* Aurora, CO: Mid-continent Research for Education and Learning. Online database: http://www.mcrel.org/standards-benchmarks

Literature Circles

. . . . ▶

Materials

- reproducibles on pages 12–20
- multiple copies of different books
- index cards
- colored markers and pencils
- Internet access (optional)

What Is a Literature Circle?

At its core, a literature circle is a small group of students who meet on a regular, predictable schedule to read and discuss a book they've selected. Each student plays a specific role in the discussion, and the teacher acts as a facilitator rather than as an active participant. The goal of literature circles is to generate animated, informal, spontaneous conversations that encourage a lifelong love of reading.

Directions

1. Choose several books for which you can find multiple copies.

2. Hold a brief book talk with your class. Show students the covers of the books and read a synopsis of each. Do not impose your feelings on the discussion, and do not allow students to discuss their views with each other at this time.

3. Give each student an index card and have them write down, in order of preference, which books they would most like to read.

4. Collect the cards and divide the class into reading groups based on their preferences. Try to allow everyone to read one of their top two or three choices. You can use the LITERATURE

Teacher Tip

When you're choosing the stories for the literature circles to read, consider selecting different texts on the same theme, by the same author, or in the same genre. This will encourage group discussions as a culminating activity once the literature circles have finished discussing their individual books. And it might entice students to read books that other groups have read.

CIRCLE PLANNING GUIDE template (page 12) to help you organize the groups.

5. Assign each student a different role to perform, or allow students to choose their own roles. (See the list of roles and responsibilities below.) These roles can rotate from meeting to meeting. Depending on the number of students in each group, you may have to combine or eliminate responsibilities or assign more than one student to a given role.

6. Vary the reading styles, allowing students to read alone, in pairs, or in groups. You can give them time to read in class, or you can ask that they read for homework. You can set daily page goals, or you can have students set these goals in their separate groups.

7. As the students read, have them complete the graphic organizer that corresponds to the role they've chosen. They will bring these completed forms to each of their meetings. You can also require students to make regular entries in their reading journals. (See the Teacher Tip on page 11.)

8. Select circle meeting dates. Allow circles to meet for a specific amount of time on a regular, predictable schedule. Students should bring their completed graphic organizers to the circle and be ready to engage in an informal conversation with their peers about the book they are reading.

9. Circulate throughout the class. Listen to and evaluate the different groups, being careful not to impose your feelings on the proceedings. Be an observer rather than a questioner.

Literature Circle Roles and Responsibilities

Circle Leader—The circle leaders need to come to each meeting with at least three *thinking* questions. These questions can begin with phrases like "Why do you think . . . ?" or "How did you feel . . . ?" The questions should not ask group members to simply recall things that happened in the story but should stimulate discussions. The leaders are also responsible for keeping the group members focused and for ensuring that each group member gets a chance to contribute to the conversation. (Use the graphic organizer on page 13.)

Book Talk

"Literature circles provide a way for students to engage in critical thinking and reflection as they read, discuss, and respond to books. Collaboration is at the heart of this approach. Students reshape and add onto their understanding as they construct meaning with other readers. Finally, literature circles guide students to deeper understanding of what they read through structured discussion and extended written and artistic response."
—Katherine L. Schlick Noe and Nancy J. Johnson, *Getting Started with Literature Circles*, Christopher-Gordon Publishers, 1999.

Super Summarizer–The super summarizers need to write a brief summary of the selection their group read, including important characters and events. Have them read their summary at the beginning of the meeting to remind everyone what the selection was about. (Use they graphic organizer on page 14.)

Word Wizard–The word wizards are responsible for finding three words or idioms that are unfamiliar or used in an interesting way. They should write each word down, its page number, the sentence in which it can be found, the part of speech (as it is used in the passage), and its definition. They are also responsible for leading a group discussion about why they think the author chose these words instead of others. Each group should then choose one of the words their word wizard found and add it to the class's word wall. They can write the necessary information on an index card before taping it to the wall. (Use the graphic organizer on page 15.)

Connector–The connectors need to find relationships between the story and the real world. Is an event from the book similar to one that happened in real life? At school or home? Does it remind you of a current or historical event? How is the story's setting similar to the region in which you live? Do any of the characters remind you of someone you know? The connectors help their group understand the story better by helping them connect to it in an experiential way. (Use the graphic organizer on page 16.)

Passage Pro–Challenge the passage pros to locate three sentences or short sections of text they think are particularly well written, interesting, funny, scary, beautiful, important, confusing, or otherwise worth discussing. Have them write the passage, the page number on which it can be found, and the reason they chose it. (Use the graphic organizer on page 17.)

Journaler–The journalers are responsible for reporting on the passage in a visual way. Have them sketch two key scenes from the selection their group read and explain why those scenes are important. The journalers will also create a graphic organizer that highlights some element of the story—using a Venn diagram, a story elements map, a character map, and so on. (Use the graphic organizer on page 18.)

Teacher Tip

Pair students of different reading levels and allow them to take turns reading their books aloud to each other. Encourage them to help each other work on their graphic organizers before meeting in their literature circles.

Background Investigator–Invite the background investigators to use the Internet or nonfiction books to help their literature circle gain a deeper understanding of some element of the book. What is the history of the book? When was it published? Is the story based on an old folktale? Who is the author? Where did he or she get the idea for this book? Did the author write any other stories? Are there any other books on this topic? What jobs do the characters have? To what culture do the characters belong? What is the setting of the story like? (Use the graphic organizer on page 19.)

Travel Tracker–The travel trackers trace the movements and changes of the characters. Instruct them to look at ways in which the characters change physically, emotionally, psychologically, spiritually, and so on. If the characters move around a lot, the travel tracker can draw a series of pictures or maps that shows where the characters were and where they are going. If the characters mature over the course of the story, the travel tracker can write a series of paragraphs that describe this growth. (Use the graphic organizer on page 20.)

Teacher Tip

Ask students to keep a journal in which they write about their experiences in the literature circles. Give them 10 to 15 minutes to record their thoughts after each meeting. Students can write about things that were discussed, something they learned, how the discussion made them feel, connections they discovered between the book and their own life, something funny that happened while the group was talking, and so on. You can ask them to respond with a drawing, a graphic organizer, or a paragraph.

Literature Circle Planning Guide

Fill out this planning guide for each literature circle to help you keep track of group members and assigned roles.

_____

(Title of Book)

_____

(Author)

Literature Circle Members	Role
1.	
2.	
3.	
4.	
5.	
6.	
7.	
8.	

Take notes of things you want this group to accomplish for the next session.

Session 1: _____

Session 2: _____

Session 3: _____

Session 4: _____

Session 5: _____

Session 6: _____

ROLE: Circle Leader

Write three *thinking* questions to get the group talking. These questions can begin with phrases like "Why do you think . . . ?" or "How did you feel when . . . ?" or "Have you ever . . . ?" You are also responsible for keeping the group members focused and making sure everyone has a chance to talk.

Question 1:

_____

_____

_____

_____

_____

_____

Question 2:

_____

_____

_____

_____

_____

_____

Question 3:

_____

_____

_____

_____

_____

_____

ROLE: *Super Summarizer*

Write a brief summary of the selection your group read. Include important characters and events. Be prepared to read the summary when your group meets. Write one *thinking* question about something that happened in the selection that you would like to discuss with your group.

Summary:

_____
_____
_____
_____
_____
_____
_____
_____
_____
_____
_____
_____
_____
_____
_____

Question:

_____
_____
_____
_____
_____
_____

Name _____ Date _____

ROLE: Word Wizard

Find three words that are unfamiliar to you or are used in an interesting way. Write the word, its page number, the sentence in which it can be found, the part of speech (as it is used in the passage), and its definition. Lead a discussion about why you think the author chose these words instead of others.

Word: **Page number:**

Sentence:

Part of speech:

Definition:

Word: **Page number:**

Sentence:

Part of speech:

Definition:

Word: **Page number:**

Sentence:

Part of speech:

Definition:

ROLE: Connector

Find connections between things that happened in the story and things in real life. Is an event from the book similar to one that happened in real life? At school or home? Does it remind you of a current or historical event? How does the story's setting remind you of the area in which you live? Do any of the characters remind you of someone you know? Be prepared to discuss these things with your group.

Event in Story	Real Life

Name _____ Date _____

ROLE: Passage Pro

Locate three sentences or short sections of the text that you think are particularly well written, interesting, funny, scary, beautiful, important, confusing, or otherwise worth discussing. Write the passage below, the page number on which it can be found, and the reason why you chose it.

Passage and Page Number	Why You Chose It

Name _____ Date _____

ROLE: Journaler

Sketch two key scenes from the selection your group read. Be prepared to explain why you think the scenes are important. Create a graphic organizer—such as a Venn diagram, a story elements map, or a character map—that highlights some element of the story.

Graphic Organizer

ROLE: Background Investigator

Use nonfiction books or the Internet to research an element of the book—
its history, author, setting, theme, characters, and so on. Write about your
discoveries in the space below.

Things I Learned:

_____

_____

_____

_____

_____

_____

_____

_____

_____

_____

_____

_____

Sketches and Notes:

ROLE: Travel Tracker

Use the graphic organizer below to trace the movement of and change in the characters. If the characters move around a lot, draw a series of pictures or maps that shows where the characters were and where they are. If a character grows or changes, write a series of paragraphs that describe this growth.

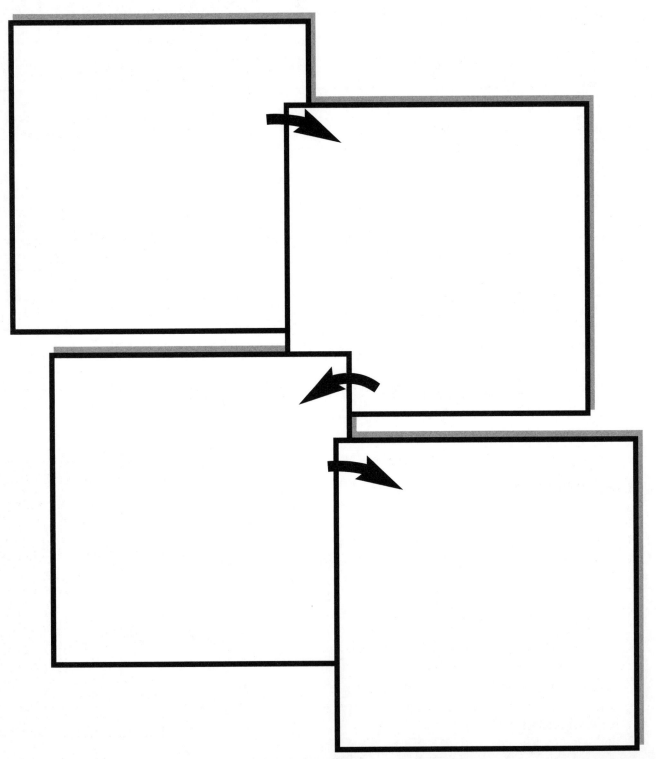

What Makes a Book?

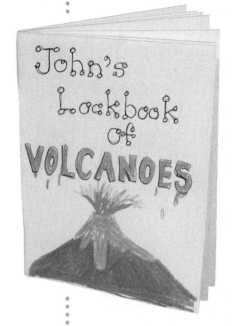

Materials

- PARTS OF A BOOK reproducible (page 24)
- $8\frac{1}{2}$- by 11-inch sheets of white copier paper
- scissors
- rulers
- colored markers and pencils
- sample books and textbooks

Purpose

Students will identify the various parts of a book, learn where they are located, and use this knowledge to create a nonfiction "lockbook" based on research they conducted.

Making the Lockbook

1. Pass out the PARTS OF A BOOK reproducible and review it with the class. Use sample books and textbooks to show examples of the different parts of books.

2. Have students cut two sheets of copier paper in half widthwise.

3. Instruct students to stack three of the half sheets and fold them in half widthwise. Then ask them to place a small pencil mark on the folded edge $1\frac{3}{8}$ inches from the top and bottom edges of the top sheet.

4. Ask students to open up the pages. Then have them cut slits in the sheets along the folded edge. The slits should extend from the top and bottom edges to just beyond the pencil marks.

Teacher Tip

If you want students to make longer lockbooks, have them feed additional sheets of paper through the sheet that has a hole in the center. This would allow students to include more chapters, or longer chapters, in their lockbook.

5. Have students fold the remaining half-sheet in half widthwise and again make pencil marks 1⅜ inches from the top and bottom edges. Then have them cut a slit in the center of the sheet, from one pencil mark to the other.

6. Ask students to keep the three identically cut sheets stacked on top of each other. Have them curl the left sides of the sheets into a cylinder and feed them through the hole in the fourth sheet.

7. Have students open up the sheets so they lock into place. They can then fold the pages into a book. Students will now each have a 16-page lockbook.

Using the Lockbook

1. Ask students to go to the library and find five books each, related to a subject that interests them. (Or you could assign the topic they are to research.)

2. After students have gathered information about their topics, have them complete steps 3–15 to create a lockbook that features the different parts of a book.

3. Instruct students to create a cover for their lockbooks. The cover should include a title and illustration related to the topic they researched, as well as their name (such as, "*The Lockbook of Bugs*, written and illustrated by John Doe").

4. Ask students to open the lockbook. The page directly following the cover should be left blank; this is the inside front cover. The first right-hand page is the title page. Instruct students to write the title of the book and their name in the center of the page. At the bottom of the page have them write the name of their publisher (a name they will create) and the city in which the book was "published."

5. The page directly following the title page is the copyright page. Have students write the copyright symbol, the year, and the phrase "by [student's name]." This can be followed by the phrase "Printed in the U.S.A."

6. The page to the right of the copyright page is the dedication page. Ask students to write a dedication on this page. Show

Teacher Tip

Students can use a glue stick to glue a sheet of construction paper around the cover. Then they can trim the construction paper so there is a half-inch border around the pages. This makes for a more polished and durable lockbook.

them several examples of dedications from different books to give them some ideas.

7. The left-hand page following the dedication page should be left blank.

8. The table of contents should be on the next right-hand page. This will include the page numbers for the preface, chapters, glossary, index, and bibliography. Students might want to finish the table of contents *after* they complete the rest of the book.

9. The page following the table of contents will be page 6. This should be the first page number in the lockbook, as the previous pages are generally not numbered in books. Ask students to write the number 6 at the bottom of this page. They can also write the page numbers for pages 7–13.

10. On page 6, have students write the word "Preface" and include a short introductory essay about the topic they chose to research—its significance and its appeal.

11. Pages 7, 8, and 9 should be titled Chapter 1, Chapter 2, and Chapter 3, respectively. On these three pages, have students write paragraphs that convey information about three aspects of the topic they researched.

12. Ask students to write the word "Glossary" at the top of page 11, followed by five unfamiliar words related to their topic. Instruct them to also include the definition of each word on this page.

13. Ask students to write the word "Index" at the top of page 12, followed by an alphabetical listing of key words and subjects included in Chapters 1–3. Next to each word or phrase, have students include the page number on which each can be found.

14. Instruct students to write the word "Bibliography" at the top of page 13 and include a list of the five resources they used to conduct their research. There are many acceptable styles for writing a bibliography. If you don't have a favored style, do a Web search to find the one you'd like students to use, or use the suggested style shown in the Teacher's Tip box at right.

15. Have students write a paragraph on the back cover that describes the book's contents.

Teacher Tip

Here is a suggested style for bibliographies that students can use in their lockbooks.

Books
Author's surname, author's first name, year of publication, *title of book in italics*, publisher, place of publication.

Encyclopedias
Title of book in italics, year of publication, publisher, place of publication, volume number, page numbers.

Magazine Articles
Author's surname, author's first name, year of publication, "title of article," *magazine name in italics*, month/volume/ issue number, page numbers.

Internet
Author's surname, author's first name, year of publication, *title of article in italics*, Internet address of article, date of access.

Parts of a Book

Cover	the front and back panels that protect the interior pages
Spine	the hinged back of the book that faces out when the book is on a bookshelf
Author	the person who wrote the book
Title	the name of the book
Illustrator	the person who drew the pictures in the book
Title Page	the page at the beginning of the book that includes the title, author, and publisher
Place of Publication	the city where the book was published
Publisher	the company that produced the book
Copyright Page	the page where the copyright date can be found
Dedication Page	the place where the author dedicates the book to someone
Table of Contents	a list of the book's contents, arranged by chapter
Preface	a short introductory essay preceding the text of a book and usually written by the author
Introduction	the opening section of a book that helps the reader understand the body of text
Body	the main text of the book
Glossary	a list of words and definitions at the end of a book
Index	a list of names and subjects in alphabetical order at the end of the book
Bibliography	a list of titles (along with author, publication date, place of publication, page numbers reference) used by an author in preparing the book

What's in a Name?

Name _Stephen Hancock_ **Date** _October 6_

What's in a Name?

Predict what you think will happen in the story based on the title of the book, the cover art, and the information contained on the back cover.

Title of Book: _A Year Down Yonder by Richard Peck_

Who?	Where?	When?	What?	Why?	How?
People from the South	Mississippi or Louisiana	1930s	Someone will face racism when they spend a year down south.	Blacks and whites didn't get along in the 1930s.	A black boy and a white boy will become friends and teach their parents to get along.
A girl and a woman	In the Plains States	1930s	A girl has to spend a year in a rural area.	I think the girl will be bored because there are no other kids.	The girl will learn to become friends with the old lady.
A 15-year old girl and her grandma.	Illinois	1930s	Mary Alice will find adventures while living with her grandmother.	Grandma always stirs things up with her neighbors.	The girl and grandmother work together to help the neighbors.

Materials

- WHAT'S IN A NAME graphic organizer (page 26)

Purpose

Students will make, confirm, and revise simple predictions about what will be found in a text based on the book's cover.

Directions

1. Pass out a copy of the WHAT'S IN A NAME graphic organizer to each student.

2. Write the title of a novel you're going to read on the board.

3. Ask students to fill out the top part of the organizer based on the title alone. *Who* do they think is the main character in the story? *Where* does the story take place? *When* is the story set? *What* do they think will happen in the story? *Why* does the major problem in the story occur? *How* is this problem solved?

4. Show students the cover art. Ask them to adjust their predictions based on this new information. Have students write their new predictions in the center part of the organizer.

5. Read the written information on the back cover of the novel to the class. Ask students to adjust their predictions based on this new information. Have them write their new predictions in the bottom part of the organizer.

6. Discuss the predictions and the adjustments that students made. Then begin reading the novel.

Teacher Tip

Help students develop prediction skills by reading out loud an action comic from your local paper for a few weeks. Each day, invite students to predict what will happen in the next day's comic. Ask students to support their predictions with evidence: story line, character traits, dialogue, illustrations, and personal experience.

Name _____

Date _____

What's in a Name?

Predict what you think will happen in the story based on the title of the book, the cover art, and the information contained on the back cover.

_____
(Title and Author of Book)

	Who?	Where?	When?	What?	Why?	How?
TITLE						
ART						
INFO						

On the Cover

Materials

- selection of class novels
- 11- by 24-inch precut sheets of oaktag or white construction paper
- rulers
- scissors
- colored markers and pencils

Purpose

Students will learn about the elements of a book's cover and how these elements influence readers' expectations.

Directions

1. Read the titles of five novels to the class without showing them the covers. Ask students to tell you which book they would most like to read. Ask them why they chose the books they did. Record the votes on the board.

2. Show students the covers of the five books. Ask students if any of them would like to change their vote. Discuss elements of a good cover illustration.

3. Read the descriptions of the stories that appear on the back covers or inside flaps. Ask students if any of them would like to change their vote. Discuss the ways in which each description "sells" the book.

4. Discuss the elements of a book's cover—the title, author, illustrator, cover illustration, description of story, author's and illustrator's bio, and so forth.

5. Read the book that received the most votes.

6. After you finish reading the novel, give each student a sheet of oaktag or white construction paper. (Oaktag is more durable and markers are less likely to bleed through.)

Teacher Tip

Create a freestanding display of the finished book covers on a countertop in the classroom, or tack the covers to a bulletin board in the hall.

7. Have students draw a pencil line 4 inches from the left side and another one 11 inches from the left side.

8. Ask them to draw a pencil line 4 inches from the right side and another one 11 inches from the right side. The paper should now look like the illustration to the right.

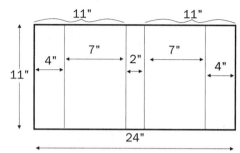

9. Instruct students to fold the paper inward along the 4-inch guidelines.

10. Have students fold the paper inward along the 11-inch guidelines so that it looks like a book jacket (see example on page 27).

11. Invite students to design a new cover for the book. On the front cover, have them draw an illustration. Remind them to include the author's name.

12. Ask students to write a paragraph on the back cover that would catch readers' attention and make them want to read the book. The paragraph should not give away any major plot points.

13. On the spine of the book, have students use decorative lettering to write the title and the author's name. Have them write the publisher's name at the bottom of the panel.

14. On the inside front and back flaps, students will write a short biography of the author. Where is she from? What other books did she write? Where did she get the idea for this book? Allow students to use the Internet to find out information about the author.

15. On the interior panels, students can write a book report that gives a brief summary, describes things they liked and/or disliked about the book, discusses problems and solutions in the story, relates favorite passages or moments, interprets symbolism, discusses important characters, and so on.

Cut-Up Conferences

Materials

- a copy of the first chapter of a novel
- scissors
- Cut-Up Conferences graphic organizer (page 30)

Purpose

Students will make predictions about a novel based on short passages from the first chapter.

Directions

1. Make a copy of the first chapter of a novel the class is about to read, and cut it into as many sections as there are students in the class.

2. Give each student a section and allow them time to read it to themselves.

3. Then ask students to meet in pairs for two-minute periods to discuss the content of their sections. Have students switch partners every two minutes, until they've each met with six different partners.

4. Pass out a copy of the Cut-Up Conferences graphic organizer to each student.

5. Ask students to fill it out based on the information they gathered during their conferences.

6. After students have completed their graphic organizers, discuss the different predictions as a class.

7. Finally, read the chapter aloud.

8. Give students time to reflect on the differences between their original predictions and what actually happened in the chapter.

Book Talk

"Predicting involves more than trying to figure out what happens next. As kids find evidence to form hunches, they also ask questions, recall facts, reread, skim, infer, draw conclusions, and, ultimately, comprehend the text more fully."
—Laura Robb, "Reading Clinic: Use Prediction to Help Kids Think Deeply About Books," *Instructor Magazine*, October 1996.

Cut-Up Conferences

In the graphic organizer below, write information that you learned during the cut-up conferences about the plot, setting, characters, and events in the chapter. If you are unsure of something, answer the questions based on your *predictions*. Remember, there are no wrong predictions.

Describe the main character. What does he or she want? What does he or she do?	Describe the minor characters. What is their relationship to the main character?	Describe the setting. When and where does the story take place? What role do you think the setting will play?
Who is telling the story? In what voice is it told?	How would you describe the mood and tone of the book?	What do you think the major problem in the book will be?

In the bottom three panels of the grid, describe three events you think will happen in this chapter.

Before and After

Materials

- copies of illustrations from a textbook or other nonfiction book

Purpose

Students will make predictions about the causes and effects of a nonfiction event on the basis of an illustration.

Directions

1. Copy illustrations from a section of a textbook (or other non-fiction book) the class is about to read that show moments of action or significance. The pictures should feature several people (such as colonists throwing boxes of tea into Boston Harbor or George Washington and his troops crossing the Delaware River).

2. Divide the class into groups that have as many members as there are people in the illustration they're given.

3. Give each group a picture. They should study the picture and discuss what they think happened immediately before and immediately after the moment shown.

4. Give each group a few minutes to plan an improvised scene that bookends the action in the picture. *What events led up to the moment shown? What happened afterwards?* The group should freeze in the middle of their scene for a few seconds at the point where the picture was taken/drawn.

5. Read the textbook passage after the scenes have been presented to see how the illustrations illuminate the events and to see what *really* happened before and after the illustrated scene.

Teacher Tip

Encourage creative thinking and deductive reasoning before reading a fiction book. Show students pictures or illustrations from the book. Have groups create a scene that imagines circum-stances that may have lead up to—and resulted from—the event shown in one of the pictures. Then read the chapter to see how the author envisioned the story.

Who, What, and Where?

Materials

- WHO, WHAT, AND WHERE? cards (pages 33–35)
- scissors

Purpose

Students will incorporate the story elements of character, setting, and plot into a simple and fun presentation before reading.

Directions

1. Make a copy of the WHO, WHAT, AND WHERE? cards on pages 33–35. Cut out the cards.

2. Divide the class into pairs.

3. Have each pair pick two character cards, one setting card, and one plot card.

4. Give students five minutes to devise a one- or two-minute scene that combines the characters, the setting, and the plot.

5. Invite the pairs to improvise their short scene. Tell the students that they should not specifically mention the types of characters they are portraying or the setting in which the scene is set. (For example, if a pirate is at a football game, the actor could say, "Arrrgh! Don't fumble the ball, matey!" rather than "What a great football game!")

6. After each scene is presented, ask the rest of the class if they could guess the two characters represented, the setting, and the basic plot.

7. End the class with a review of the basic story elements.

Teacher Tip

Newspaper articles provide a ready-made way to discuss basic story elements. Cut out newspaper articles and give one to each student. Have them read their articles and highlight the story elements—Character: Who is the article about? Plot: What is the article about? Setting: Where and when does it take place? Problem: Why is the article news-worthy? Solution: How was the problem resolved, or how is it being resolved?

Who, What, and Where? Character Cards

CHARACTER CARD

pirate

CHARACTER CARD

ballet dancer

CHARACTER CARD

clown

CHARACTER CARD

chef

CHARACTER CARD

talking monkey

CHARACTER CARD

spy

CHARACTER CARD

president

CHARACTER CARD

two-year-old

CHARACTER CARD

superhero

CHARACTER CARD

elderly person

CHARACTER CARD

prisoner

CHARACTER CARD

tourist

CHARACTER CARD

mad scientist

CHARACTER CARD

artist

CHARACTER CARD

rock singer

CHARACTER CARD

professional wrestler

CHARACTER CARD

vampire

CHARACTER CARD

used car salesman

Who, What, and Where? Plot Cards

PLOT CARD	PLOT CARD	PLOT CARD
helping someone who is lost	investigating a robbery	auditioning for a show
nursing a sick person	finding a lost pet	exploring unfamiliar territory
searching for buried treasure	putting out a fire	trying to cook dinner
teaching a lesson	cleaning a messy area	meeting a long-lost friend
comforting a sad friend	overpowering a bully	studying for an important test
solving a mystery	surprising a friend with a gift	hiding from an enemy

Who, What, and Where? Setting Cards

SETTING CARD

in a desert

SETTING CARD

at a circus

SETTING CARD

on a wagon train

SETTING CARD

at a wedding

SETTING CARD

at a football game

SETTING CARD

in a classroom

SETTING CARD

on a beach

SETTING CARD

in a fancy restaurant

SETTING CARD

on a spaceship

SETTING CARD

in a blizzard

SETTING CARD

at an amusement park

SETTING CARD

in a library

SETTING CARD

in a dentist's office

SETTING CARD

in ancient Egypt

SETTING CARD

in a haunted house

SETTING CARD

at the zoo

SETTING CARD

in the jungle

SETTING CARD

on an African safari

Opposites Attract

Purpose

Students will identify characteristics of protagonists and antagonists.

Directions

1. Divide the class in half and explain that a protagonist is a good guy and an antagonist is a bad guy.

2. Ask one half to brainstorm a list of famous or stereotypical protagonists (Superman, and angel, Harry Potter). Have them create a second list of characteristics of these protagonists (good, heroic, trustworthy, and so on).

3. Instruct the other half to brainstorm a list of famous or stereotypical antagonists (a robber, a bully, Darth Vadar). Have them create a list of characteristics of these antagonists (dishonest, mean, evil, and so on).

4. Have the students in each group pick a protagonist or an antagonist.

5. Match students up randomly and ask them to create a one-minute improvisation that features the protagonist and the antagonist in a situation such as meeting for a cup of coffee, sharing a cab, sitting in a doctor's waiting room, and so on.

6. Invite each pair of students to perform their improv for the class.

7. Read a short story to the class and ask them to identify the protagonist and antagonist. Ask students to name traits these characters exhibited in the story.

Book Talk

"Play is democratic! Anyone can play! Everyone can learn through playing! Play touches and stimulates vitality, awakening the whole person—mind and body, intelligence and creativity, spontaneity and intuition—when all, teacher and students together, are attentive to the moment."
—Viola Spolin, *Theater Games for the Classroom*, Northwestern University Press, 1986.

Read-Around Genre Reports

Materials

- examples of books from different genres
- 8- by 30-inch sheets of white bulletin board paper
- rulers
- colored markers and pencils
- tape
- hole punches
- scissors
- string

Purpose

Students will learn about the basic characteristics of familiar genres.

Directions

1. Take your class on a "field trip" to the school's library or the local public library. (You might even consider asking the librarian to help you teach this lesson.)

2. Host a book talk with your students, showing them examples of books from different genres and asking them to name the different genres' characteristics. (A list of genres and their characteristics can be found on page 39.)

3. Ask students to each select a genre, and tell them that they are going to do a mini-report on it.

4. Allow students to check out a few examples of books from their chosen genre.

5. When you return to the classroom, tell students to examine their books' covers, scan the text, and look at the pictures, if any. Tell them to jot down characteristics of the genre they chose, based on their findings. Provide help if needed.

Teacher Tip

Describe ways in which the genres can overlap. For example, historical fiction can also be a mystery. Or a western can also contain elements of an adventure novel.

6. Give each student a sheet of white bulletin board paper.

7. Ask students to draw a 7-inch square one-half inch from the left edge.

8. Tell students to draw a picture in the square that is representative of a scene from the genre they chose; for example, a student who chose to report on science fiction might draw a picture of a rocket flying through space, an alien planet, or a robot.

9. Across the top of the right side of the paper, ask students to write the name of the genre they researched.

10. Have students include the following three items below the title:

- a word web featuring characteristics of the genre
- a list of five books and authors from the genre
- a paragraph describing why the student chose the genre and what he or she finds most interesting about it

Encourage students to use a ruler to neatly organize and lay out this information. Have them draw writing lines in pencil, write the text in ink, and then erase the pencil marks.

11. After students have finished writing their reports, ask them to curl the paper into a cylinder and tape it.

12. Then show students how to punch four holes in the top of the report, tie strings to each of the holes, and connect the strings to a central string.

13. Invite students to give a short oral report about their genre. They should describe the things they like about it and share information they included on their read-around report.

14. Hang the reports from the ceiling so they are able to spin freely in the breeze.

Cross-Curriculum

Invite students to create read-around reports in science class that focus on cyclical processes such as the water cycle, the life cycle of an oak tree, or the metamorphosis of an insect. Ask students to illustrate each phase of the process. As the reports spin, they mirror the cyclical nature of the processes described.

Suggested Genres and Characteristics

Adventure/Suspense—travel, realistic settings, journeys, quests, physical action, tense, heroic main character, big obstacles, page-turner, cliffhangers at end of each chapter, realistic characters and setting, fast paced, exciting, danger, villains, twists and turns

Biographies—the story of a person's life, factual, autobiography, nonfiction, feats and accomplishments, major events

Drama—realistic characters, slow pace, happy or sad ending, strong emotions, serious

Fantasy—magical creatures, different worlds, dragons, magic, elves, fairies, unicorns, unreal, animals with human characteristics

Folktales, Fables, and Fairy Tales—passed down through generations, talking animals, moral lessons, princesses, magical

Historical Fiction—based on real events or time, set in the past, strong sense of place and time, blend of actual and made-up elements

Horror—scary, monsters or other scary creatures, page-turner, aliens, nightmares

Humor—funny, jokes, comedy, absurd situations, zany characters

Mystery—puzzles, clues, sleuths, detectives, red herrings, crime, who-done-it, suspicious characters, suspense, solution, twists, surprises, spies

Myths and Legends—explain how natural things (such as the world or the sun) were created, magical, giants, gods and goddesses, stories from long ago

Nonfiction—informational, factual, how things work, history, science, biographies

Picture Books—illustrations, easy to read, short

Poetry—verse, rhyme, figurative language, humorous or serious, lyrical or narrative, rhythm, meter, imagery

Romance—love, happy ending, adventure, heroes and heroines, usually short in length, easy to read, obstacles get in the way of the boy and girl getting together, villains

Science Fiction—technology, future, space, distant worlds, danger, aliens, robots, time travel, computers, scientists, laboratories, spaceships

Tall Tales—far-fetched, exaggeration, larger-than-life characters, legendary characters, heroes, superhuman abilities, funny, lots of action

Westerns—cowboys, outlaws, Native Americans, Old West, frontier towns, prairies, buffalo, horses, wagon trains

You're Just My Type

Book Talk

"The analysis of different types of literature promotes cognitive development because it gives students an opportunity to apply similar skills and strategies, such as identifying themes discussed in one genre—fiction, for example—to other genres like poetry, reports, descriptive pieces, and plays."
—Carl B. Smith, "The Role of Different Literary Genres," *The Reading Teacher*, Vol. 44, 1991.

Materials

- sheets of white legal-size paper
- rulers
- colored markers and pencils

Purpose

Students will demonstrate a knowledge of the basic characteristics of familiar genres.

Directions

1. Give each student a sheet of white legal-size paper.

2. Have students fold the bottom edge upward so that it creates a 1-inch lip.

3. Tell them to fold the top edge downward and tuck it behind the lip at the bottom. This creates something that looks like a matchbook.

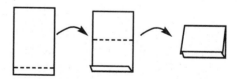

4. Have each student choose a different literary genre, if possible. A list of genres can be found on page 39.

5. Instruct students to write the name of the genre on the lower flap.

6. On the outside of the upper flap, have students draw a representative scene from a book of that genre; for example, for the mystery genre the student might draw a detective holding a magnifying glass or a burglar hiding in the shadows.

7. Have students lift the upper flap. Inside the matchbook, have them create a word web that lists words and phrases related to the genre. See the example below.

8. After students have completed their genre studies, collect them and hang them on a bulletin board under a banner that reads YOU'RE JUST MY TYPE OF BOOK!

Teacher Tip

There are many genres of books. Find enough so that each student can report on a different one. This will create a diverse display of genres for the bulletin board. Allow students to use trade books and the Internet to conduct their research.

Hot, Hot, Hot!

Materials
- eraser
- paper cup

Purpose

Students will analyze the way in which a story builds toward a climax.

Directions

1. Ask students to sit in a circle. Hand an object—such as an eraser—to one of the students.

2. Tell them to pass the object around the circle. When they're done, ask them to describe what happened. (Not very exciting, huh?)

3. Tell them to pass the object around the circle again, only this time have them pretend that the object gets a little hotter each time it is passed to another person; it should be scalding hot by the time it reaches the last person. Each person should hold the object for at least five seconds before passing it to the next person. When they're done, ask the students to describe what happened.

4. Repeat this activity with a paper cup or soda bottle. Ask each student to smell what's in the cup. The contents get stinkier each time the cup is passed until the stench becomes unbearable.

5. Discuss how this exercise is similar to the plot of a good book. An author must increase the stakes over the course of the story in order to keep the reader interested. If there is no rising action, the reader becomes bored and uninterested in the story being told.

Teacher Tip

To convey the idea that action rises and falls throughout a story, you could guide the "temperature" of the object as it is being passed around the circle by saying, "It's getting hotter, hotter, hotter; it's cooling off a little; now it's getting hotter; it's boiling," and so on. The students should base their reactions both on your words and on the actions of the previous students.

Five Words

Materials

- index cards

Purpose

Students will learn the meanings of new vocabulary words and use them in the context of a short, improvised scene.

Directions

1. Divide all of the new vocabulary words that students will have to learn into sets of five; these words can come from a textbook or nonfiction thematic unit or from a novel the students are about to read.

2. Write each set of five words on an index card.

3. Divide your class into groups of four or five and give each group an index card.

4. Instruct the groups to look up the definitions for the words on their card and write them down.

5. Ask the groups to create a two-minute scene that has a beginning, a middle, and an end, and that uses the five words in such a way that their meanings are clear.

6. After each group has had a chance to perform their scene, ask the rest of the class if they can tell you the meanings of the vocabulary words the group used. Discuss and define further if necessary.

7. As you come across each word while reading the textbook or novel, reflect back on this activity. Discuss the way the word was used in the skit and how it is used in the text.

Teacher Tip

Creative dramatics promotes social skills because these activities stimulate discussions within groups as students work together to solve a problem. The more often you have students perform in front of their peers, the more confident they will become with public speaking.

Easy Book Making

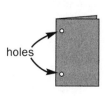

Purpose

Students will construct bound books in which they can write and illustrate stories for the class library.

Directions

1. Ask students to find straight, solid sticks from trees or bushes that measure approximately 7 or 8 inches. These will be used to bind the books they'll be making. You could also have them use thin wooden shish kebab skewers.

2. Make double-sided copies of the LINED PAGE writing template and give four copies to each student.

3. Give each student a sheet of construction paper to be used as the cover of the book.

4. Have students put the lined templates on top of the cover sheet and fold them in half, like a book.

fold here

5. Show students how to punch two holes about ¼ inch from the folded edge through all the layers of the paper. The holes should be about 1½ inches from the top and bottom edges.

holes

Teacher Tip

Reading and writing are flip sides of a coin. Improving skills in one sharpens them in the other. Encourage writing in your reading classroom by inviting students to write their own books—diaries, autobiographies, travelogues, response logs, science journals, fictional stories, and so on. Invite students to read their stories aloud or to add their handmade books to the class library for others to enjoy.

6. Have students thread both ends of a length of ribbon, raffia, or string through the bottom hole. Then tell them to insert the stick or skewer into the loop to hold it in place before pulling the looped end through.

7. Show students how to pull the two ends of the ribbon through the top hole, from behind, and tightly tie it around the top of the stick to secure it in place. (An elastic band can be used in place of the ribbon. Feed one end of the band through the bottom hole and insert the stick through the exposed loop. Then feed the other end of the band through the top hole and pull it so it loops over the stick. The elastic band will tighten and hold the stick in place.)

8. Have students write a story on the lined pages and draw pictures in the upper section of each page. When their story is complete, they can write the title on the cover.

Teacher Tip

Instead of having students illustrate the stories they wrote, challenge them to photograph friends and family members posing as characters in scenes from the stories. Students can then glue the photos in their books to accompany their writing.

Cross-Curriculum

Encourage students to create an illustrated comic book of the life of a significant figure, a historical event, or a biographical episode from their own lives.

What's My Purpose?

Materials

- WHAT'S MY PURPOSE? cards (pages 48–49)
- paper bag

Purpose

Students will identify the purpose and intended audience of different kinds of writing.

Directions

1. Make a copy of the WHAT'S MY PURPOSE? cards and cut them out.

2. Put the cards into a paper bag and shake them.

3. Ask a volunteer to pick a card from the bag and to pretend he or she is reading the type of item named on the card without saying what the item is. For example, if she picks "road map," she might say, "Let's see, I have to go three miles along Elm Street, and then turn left onto Colonial Drive. Travel three blocks, and turn left on Highway 603. Get off at exit 15."

4. Ask the other students to guess the type of writing the volunteer is reading and what its purpose is. For example, ask the class, "What are reasons someone would read a road map?" Remind them that there might be more than one purpose.

5. Then ask students to identify the intended audience(s) for the writing purpose mentioned.

6. After all of the cards have been drawn and performed, ask the students to identify how understanding the purpose and audience for a piece of writing can make them more effective readers and writers.

Teacher Tip

Collect examples of each of the types of writing listed on the cards (or ask students to go on a scavenger hunt to find as many different examples as possible). Ask each student to write a short report on a different kind of writing, its purpose, and its intended audience. Hang the writing examples and the reports on a bulletin board under a banner that reads WHAT'S MY PURPOSE?

What's My Purpose?

What's My Purpose?

a diary entry

What's My Purpose?

a joke book

What's My Purpose?

a science experiment

What's My Purpose?

a road map

What's My Purpose?

directions on
a bottle of medicine

What's My Purpose?

a social studies
textbook

What's My Purpose?

an invitation to a
birthday party

What's My Purpose?

a newspaper article

What's My Purpose?

a travel guide

What's My Purpose?

a movie review

What's My Purpose?

a biography

What's My Purpose?

a letter to a friend

What's My Purpose?

a postcard

What's My Purpose?

a script for a
puppet show

What's My Purpose?

a dictionary

What's My Purpose?

a letter of complaint

What's My Purpose?

a baby announcement

What's My Purpose?

a letter of apology

What's My Purpose?

What's My Purpose?	What's My Purpose?	What's My Purpose?
a weather report	directions for putting together a model	a grocery list
a comic strip	a crossword puzzle	the directions for a board game
an encyclopedia	a recipe	a children's book
a report card	an obituary	a bird watcher's field guide
song lyrics	a TV guide	a rule book for a sport
a math test	a menu	sheet music for the piano

Readers Theater

Materials
- copies of stories
- highlighters or pens

What Is Readers Theater?

Readers Theater is a powerful reading strategy that exposes an audience to the full text of a story and provides an opportunity for students to analyze a text, read it aloud in front of an audience, and improve expression in their reading.

Almost any story can be used for Readers Theater, but some work better than others. The most easily adaptable stories feature lots of dialogue, a handful of characters, and a lively plot.

There are many styles of Readers Theater, but one quality that most share is that they are easy to implement. No memorization is required, and there is no need for sets, props, or costumes. All that is required are copies of the text, highlighters or pens, and a readiness to have fun.

Directions

1. Make copies of short stories or chapters from a novel that have a lot of dialogue. (Using copies allows students to highlight their lines on the manuscript.)

2. Divide the class into groups. Group sizes can vary depending on the complexity of the text. Give each group a different short story or section of text.

Teacher Tip

Use Readers Theater for an author study. Each group can adapt the short stories of a famous author—O. Henry for example—into a Readers Theater script. This way, the entire class is exposed to several pieces by a featured author, while having the opportunity to work with one piece more closely.

3. Ask students to read through the text and decide how many characters and narrators are needed. Narrators will read everything that is not in quotes, including phrases like "said the old lady" or "replied the little boy." Actors will read everything that is in quotes. (Breaking down a script in this fashion provides a perfect opportunity for students to learn about "said" phrases and how quotes are used.) If there are more characters than the group has actors, some or all students can read multiple parts, allowing them to practice expressive reading and characterization in order to convey them.

4. Ask groups to decide who will read each part, and have students highlight the part(s) they will read.

5. Instruct groups to practice reading the script to themselves, practicing vocal inflection and facial expression.

6. After practicing, students present their script to the class. Groups should stand in a line facing the audience, making sure each member can be seen. Actors can look down quickly at their script, but should try to say their line while looking at a fixed point above the heads in the audience. When the actors speak to other characters, they should not face them. Rather, they should continue looking at the fixed point as if they were looking at the other characters. If one character hands something to another character, the first student should mime handing it toward the fixed point. At the same time, the recipient should mime accepting the object from his or her fixed point.

7. Remind students to project their voices so they can be heard, to not speak too fast, to use good diction so they can be understood, and to stay in character at all times, meaning they should not giggle or fidget.

Teacher Tip

Use Readers Theater as a stepping-stone toward more formalized styles of theater. Once students become familiar with the presentational nature of Readers Theater, begin adding other theatrical elements—simple props, sets, and costumes. Allow students to stage their performance, moving around the stage and interacting with each other, while still carrying their scripts. Then, consider having students memorize their lines and staging a performance for another class or grade level.

Teacher Tip

Readers Theater can easily be adapted to all reading levels. The difficulty of the script and the size of the parts can be adjusted to ensure that all students succeed. You can also find Readers Theater scripts online. Just do a Web search for related sites.

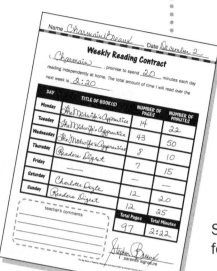

Weekly Reading Contract

Materials

- WEEKLY READING CONTRACT reproducible (page 53)
- DEAR PARENTS reproducible (pages 54–55)

Purpose

Students will implement a plan to read at home for a proposed period of time.

Directions

1. Send a copy of the DEAR PARENTS reproducible home with each student to inform parents about your at-home reading program.

2. Pass out copies of the WEEKLY READING CONTRACT to students each Monday morning.

3. Ask students to write the number of minutes they plan to spend reading each day and the total length of time they will read over the next week.

4. Tell students that each evening they should fill out the number of minutes and the number of pages they read independently that day.

5. Ask students to respond to what they've read—once a week, a few times a week, or daily—on the back of their WEEKLY READING CONTRACT. Allow them to use additional pages if necessary. (See the Reading Response Prompts on pages 57–58 for ideas.)

6. The following Sunday evening, have students add up the total number of minutes and pages they'd read the previous week. They should have a parent sign the contract.

7. Collect the contracts on Monday morning and keep them in the students' reading folders. During individual conferences, work with each student to assess his or her progress and to decide on the amount of time the student should read the following week.

Teacher Tip

Over the course of the year, check the total number of minutes each student spent reading against the total number of pages read. This is a good gauge to see if reading speed increases over time. Of course, the difficulty level of the selected stories will also affect the speed at which students read, so take this into account when you assess students' progress.

Name _____ Date _____

Weekly Reading Contract

I, _____ , promise to spend _____ minutes each day

reading independently at home. The total amount of time I will read over the

next week is _____ .

DAY	TITLE OF BOOK(S)	NUMBER OF PAGES	NUMBER OF MINUTES
Monday			
Tuesday			
Wednesday			
Thursday			
Friday			
Saturday			
Sunday			
		Total Pages	Total Minutes

Teacher's Comments

_____

_____

_____

_____

_____
Parent's Signature

Dear Parents,

Reading is the foundation of all learning, and it is one of my goals this year to ensure that your child becomes an avid, lifelong reader. You play a major role in helping your child reach his or her potential. Research in the area of child development has found that most of a child's intellectual development takes place outside the classroom. This means that children spend a great deal of time with their first and most important teachers—their parents. Indeed, as parents, your involvement in your child's learning experiences will have much to do with how well your child succeeds in school and in later life. By working together, I believe we can all help your child become the best person possible— socially, emotionally, and academically.

I am writing to introduce you to my at-home reading program and to offer suggestions for ways you can nurture a love of reading in your child. Each week your child will bring home a Weekly Reading Contract, which will list the number of minutes he or she has committed to at-home reading each day during the upcoming week. On Sunday nights, I ask that you review the completed contract with your child and sign it. Discuss the reading response your child has written on the back of his or her contract. Ask questions that prompt discussions about the books or articles your child read that week. Then have your child return the signed contract to me on Monday morning.

With all of life's distractions—hundreds of television channels, video games, megamalls, etc.—it is especially hard for today's child to choose reading as the preferred activity. Here are some ways that you can help create a literate environment in your home:

- **Be a model reader.** Let your child see you read. Read newspapers, magazines, and books of all types. Point out interesting things you read. Discuss words that sound playful. Comment on the way a writer uses language. Ask your child questions as you read. And read to your child often. A child is never too old to be read to. Reading aloud not only allows your child to hear your voice, explore the beauty of language, and learn how to be expressive, but it provides an incredible bonding experience.
- **Make regular trips to the library.** Get a library card for your child. Help your child select books. Examine the covers together. Read a few lines from each book. Read the synopsis. Look at the pictures. Let your child see that

you take reading seriously. Allow your child to choose the books he or she reads.

- **Let your child read to you.** Compliment your child on his or her reading skills. Ask general comprehension questions, but don't turn it into a lesson. Reading at home should not feel like school. Consult me if you notice any problems.

- **Provide a range of reading materials.** Fill your house with fiction and nonfiction. Check out books from the library that echo subjects and themes being taught in school. Even if your child only flips through the books, he or she will learn to turn to books for information.

- **Use reading as a reward.** Allow your child to turn the light out fifteen minutes later than usual if he or she spends the time reading in bed. Reward your child for helping you with a chore by reading to him or her for fifteen minutes.

Reading—like playing an instrument or excelling at a sport—is a skill that improves with practice. Research shows that children who read daily—whether it's newspapers, magazines, or books—are more likely to do better in school and become readers later in life. Let's work together to ensure that this happens for *your* child.

Sincerely,

Reading Response Logs

Materials

- READING RESPONSE LOG reproducibles (pages 59–60)
- sheets of three-hole-punch copier paper
- colored markers or pencils
- three-ring binders
- construction paper
- hole punch

Purpose

Students will write in response to fiction and nonfiction literature (summarize main ideas, advance judgements, make connections, and so on).

Directions

1. Look over the sample reading response prompts listed on pages 57–58. Choose one of these or create one of your own.

2. Write the prompt on one of the READING RESPONSE LOG reproducibles on pages 59–60. Use the art page if artwork is required. Use the writing page if the response is to be written.

3. Make copies of the reproducible on three-hole-punch copier paper and give a copy to each student.

4. Ask students to respond to the prompt.

5. When students complete the page, they should put it into a three-ring binder. More pages can be added as students complete them.

6. Invite students to use construction paper and colored markers to create a cover page for their reading response log. Use a hole punch to punch three holes in the construction paper so they can be added to the log.

Cross-Curriculum

Foster the use of technology in the classroom by inviting students to e-mail their reading responses to the class. Pose a question, and then allow each student time on a computer in the classroom or computer lab to answer it. Ask students to read the other responses and reply if desired. This activity can inspire a written dialogue about books among your students.

Reading Response Prompts

Type of Prompt	Sample Prompts (F–Fiction, NF–Nonfiction)
Recall	- Summarize the chapter you just read. (F/NF) - Draw a picture of the climax of the story. (F) - List five adjectives that describe the book's main character. (F/NF) - Describe the setting of the story. Illustrate it. (F/NF) - What is the major problem in the story? How is it solved? (F) - List five facts that you learned about the topic covered in the textbook or article. (NF)
Prediction	- How do you think the story will end? (F/NF) - Which character do you think will change the most by the end? (F) - Who do you think the culprit is? (F) - Based on the title, what do you think the book is about? (F/NF) - Look at the illustrations. What do they tell you about the book? (F/NF) - How do you think this conflict will be resolved? (F/NF) - Draw a picture of what you think will happen next. Describe it in a sentence. (F/NF) - How do you think the invention you researched will affect the future? (NF) - What do you think will be the result of this experiment? (NF)
Connections	- How is this book similar to another you have read by this author? (F) - Create a Venn diagram that compares the setting of this story with the area where you live. (F/NF) - What were your feelings after reading the first chapter? (F/NF) - What advice would you give a character in this book? Why? (F) - What character would you most like to be? Why? (F) - Write an e-mail that you would like to send to the author. (F/NF) - If you were a character in this book, how would it affect the plot? (F) - Describe a character's personality trait that you'd like to possess. Why do you like this trait? (F/NF) - What would you do first if you visited the city/state/country you researched? (NF) - In what ways are you similar to the famous person you researched? (NF) - Compare the historical period you investigated with the present. What are the differences and similarities? (NF) - Draw and describe an event from your life that is like an event that happened in the biography you read. (NF) - How has this invention or discovery impacted your life? (NF)

Reading Response Prompts

Type of Prompt	Sample Prompts (F–Fiction, NF–Nonfiction)
Opinion	- Why do you think the author chose the opening line he or she did? Do you like it? Did it make you want to read further? (F) - Who is your favorite character? Why? Draw a picture of this character. (F) - What do you think of the antagonist's actions? Are they right or wrong? (F) - What do you think is the most important scene in the book? Why? (F) - How would a different setting affect the story? (F) - Was the cover design effective? Did it make you want to read the book? Create a new cover design for this book. (F/NF) - Did you like the ending of the book? How would you have liked it to end? Rewrite a new ending for the book. (F) - Write a question you would like to ask the author. How do you think he or she would respond? (F/NF) - Do you agree with the point the author is making? (F/NF) - Did the graphs and diagrams help you understand the text better? (NF) - Which of the environmental issues that you read about is the most important, in your opinion? List possible solutions to this problem. (NF)
Language	- Copy a sentence from the book that you think is well written. Why do you like this sentence? Illustrate the sentence. (F) - Find examples of figurative language in the text. Write them down. (F) - What is your favorite line spoken by a character? Why do you like it? (F) - List five words from the book that you find interesting or unfamiliar. Write their definitions and use each of them in a sentence. (F/NF) - Were the directions clearly written and easy to follow? Why or why not? (NF)
Evaluation	- Did you enjoy the book? Why or why not? (F/NF) - Was the book hard or easy to read? Why? (F/NF) - What didn't you understand in the text? (I'll respond to your questions when I check your log.) (F/NF) - Would boys and girls enjoy this book equally? Support your answer. (F/NF) - Would you like to read more books by this author? Why or why not? (F/NF) - Do you think the author chose a good title for the book? Why or why not? (F/NF) - What did you learn about the time in which the story took place? (F/NF) - What do you know now that you didn't know before? (F/NF) - Describe your feelings after finishing the book or article. (F/NF)

Name _____ Date _____

Reading Response Log Art Template

Prompt: _____

_____

_____

_____

_____

_____

_____

_____

Name _____ Date _____

Reading Response Log Writing Template

Prompt: _____

_____

_____

_____

_____

_____

_____

_____

_____

_____

_____

_____

_____

_____

_____

_____

_____

_____

_____

You've Got Mail!

Materials

- cereal boxes
- scissors
- bulletin board paper
- FLAG template (page 62)
- oaktag or card stock
- tape
- colored markers and pencils
- metal brads
- glue sticks

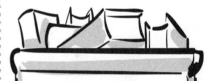

Purpose

Students will demonstrate an understanding of the concepts of problem and solution in a literary text.

Directions

1. Ask students to bring in empty cereal boxes. Boxes can vary in size and shape, but they shouldn't be too large.

2. Tell students to cut off the flaps at the open end of their box.

3. Have students wrap the boxes in bulletin board paper, leaving the open end accessible. Allow students to choose the color paper they'd like to use. This will create a more colorful bulletin board.

Book Talk

"The ultimate purpose of reading and writing is meaningful communication, and letter writing provides an authentic, reinforcing form of written communication. In addition to supporting basic literacy skills, letter writing also promotes social interaction and develops a competence that children will use throughout their lives."
—J. E. LeVine, "Writing Letters to Support Literacy," *The Reading Teacher,* Vol. 60, 2002.

4. Pass out a copy of the Flag template to each student. Instruct them to color the flag, use a glue stick to adhere it to a sheet of oaktag or card stock, and then cut out the flag.

5. Tell students to place the box in front of them horizontally. Show them how to use a metal brad to affix the flag to the upper left corner of the box's front. The flag can be raised when the box contains mail and lowered when it is empty.

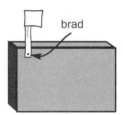

6. Have students use large, decorative lettering to write their name on the front of their mailbox.

7. Hang a banner on the bulletin board that reads You've Got Mail! Attach the mailboxes under the banner. You might want to have students make "wooden" posts out of construction paper for the mailboxes to sit on.

8. Challenge students to write a letter from the point of view of a book's main character and address it to a secondary character. In it, have students describe the major problem the main character faces in the story. They can then write a response from the secondary character's point of view that describes the solution to the main character's problem as it happened in the story.

Flag Template

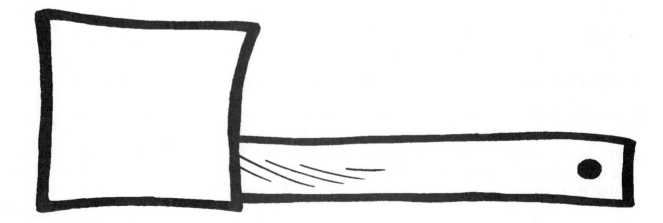

Classroom Comix

Purpose

Students will identify and sequence the main actions or events from a story or biography they are reading.

Directions

1. Make copies of the CLASSROOM COMIX template and cut them in half. Give each student a half sheet.

2. As you read a novel in class, assign a different page to each student. For homework, ask students to reread their assigned page. Students should write the page number at the top of the template, write a sentence or two describing the main idea from the selection, and draw a picture of the main idea.

3. Ask students to cut out the panel and bring it back to school.

4. Punch two holes in the top of each panel. Tie a string across a wall in your classroom. Thread the string through the panels in sequential order, adding panels each day. When the class is finished reading the story, they will have created a long comic strip that outlines the main idea from each page of the novel.

Cross-Curriculum

Ask students to use the CLASSROOM COMIX template to detail the steps in a scientific experiment or the sequence of events leading to the Revolutionary War. They can also create autobiographical comics, with each panel representing a different year in their life.

Classroom Comix

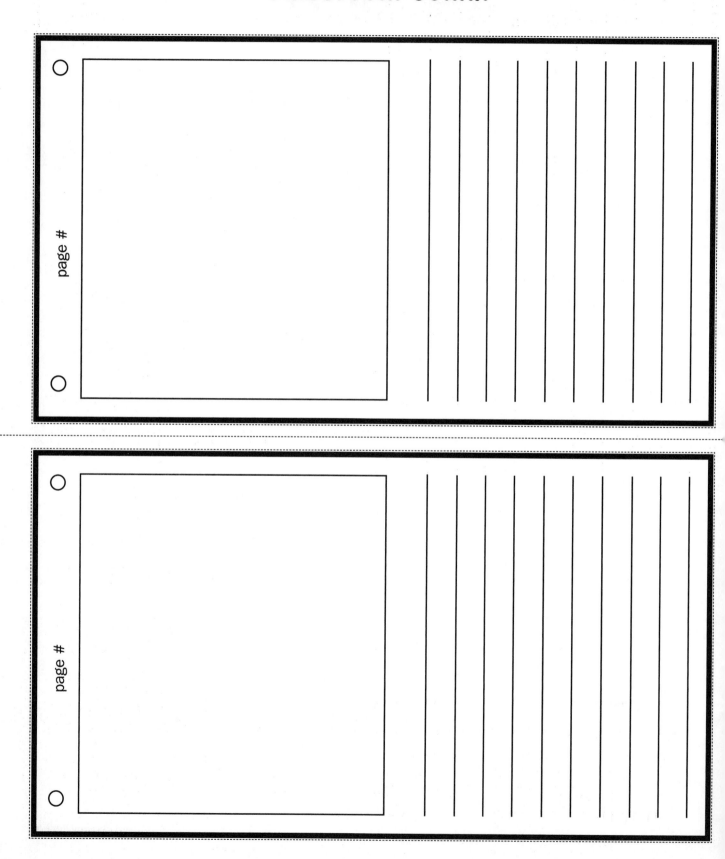

Vocabulary Card Cases

Materials

- 12- by 18-inch sheets of construction paper
- rulers
- scissors
- hole punch
- glue sticks
- colored markers and pencils
- 3- by 5-inch index cards
- tape
- 18-inch strands of yarn

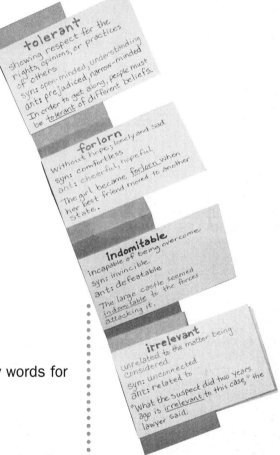

Purpose

Students will learn the meanings of new vocabulary words for a fiction or nonfiction book they are reading.

Directions

1. Ask students to cut two 2¾- by 17-inch strips of construction paper.

2. Have students fold a half-inch tab at the end of each strip.

3. Direct students to fold the two strips in half, with the tab on the inside of the fold.

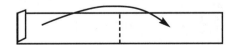

4. Have students to fold the top half of each strip back again so that it meets the crease they just made.

Teacher Tip

Students can make longer cases with room for more vocabulary words by gluing three or more strips of construction paper together.

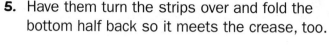

5. Have them turn the strips over and fold the bottom half back so it meets the crease, too.

6. Ask students to place the two pieces of paper next to each other so the tabs are at the top.

7. Have them put glue on one of the tabs and adhere it to the back of the other strip, to create one long accordion strip. This will be a card case for vocabulary words.

Put glue on this tab and adhere it to the back of the other strip.

8. Show students how to punch a hole in the center of the tab on their accordion cases and thread a length of yarn through the hole. Show them how to wrap one side of the yarn around the case so that an equal length of yarn hangs on each side of the closed accordion case. Have them tie a double knot in the yarn by the hole to keep it in place (see photo at right).

Punch a hole in the center of this tab, and then thread a length of yarn through it.

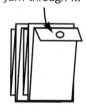

9. Assign eight vocabulary words the students will encounter in their reading, and give each student eight index cards. On the lined side of each card, have students write a vocabulary word, its definition, a synonym, an antonym, and a sentence using the word properly. On the blank side of the card, students can draw a picture illustrating the word.

10. Have students tape the left side of the index card to the left edge of one of the accordion folds on the case. The card can be lifted to reveal the back side (see illustration at right).

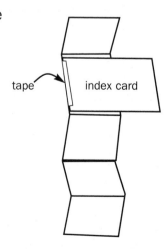

tape   index card

11. Once students have taped the eight index cards to the eight panels of the accordion case, they can close the case and tie a bow in the yarn to hold the case closed. Use the yarn to hang the projects when they are opened.

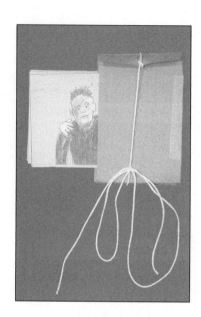

✳ Cross-Curriculum

In the language arts classroom, students can create an eight-panel accordion case that focuses on the eight major parts of speech. Each index card can feature rules, uses, and examples of nouns, verbs, pronouns, adjectives, adverbs, prepositions, conjunctions, and interjections.

Accordion Characters

Materials

- sheets of legal-size copier paper
- scissors
- colored pencils and markers

Purpose

Students will demonstrate knowledge of a fictional or real-life character's traits, development, and significance from a story or biography they are reading.

Directions

1. Give one sheet of legal-size copier paper to every two students, and have one of the students cut it in half vertically. Each student will now have one half sheet.

2. Ask students to fold the sheet in half three times. When it is opened, there will be eight panels.

3. Have students accordion fold the paper, using the creases as guides.

4. Tell students to choose a character from a novel they are reading or a real-life person they are studying. Ask them to draw the person's head on the top panel and two feet on the bottom panel. Tell them to cut away the extra paper around the head and feet.

5. Students can now design and color a body. The clothing should reflect the character or person they chose.

6. On the back of the figure, students can write a list of adjectives that describe the character, copy dialogue from the novel that reveals character traits, create a Venn diagram to compare and contrast the character with themselves, describe why they like or dislike the character, or create a timeline of significant events from the character's life.

Teacher Tip

To display the characters, hang a string across the classroom. Tie lengths of thread to the string. Tie a paper clip to the end of each piece of thread. Clip on the characters and watch them spin in the breeze.

There's No Place Like Home

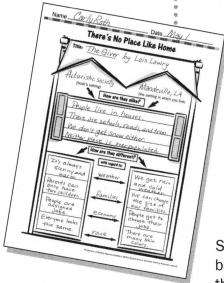

Materials

- THERE'S NO PLACE LIKE HOME graphic organizer (page 69)

Purpose

Students will examine similarities and differences between the setting of a fiction or nonfiction book they are reading and the setting in which they live.

Directions

1. Pass out copies of the THERE'S NO PLACE LIKE HOME graphic organizer to students.

2. Ask students to write the title of a novel or nonfiction text they're reading on the roof.

3. On the top left dormer, have students write the name of the text's setting. On the top right dormer, have them write the name of the setting in which they live. This can be as general or as specific as you'd like. For example, students can write the name of the city or town in which they live, the type of terrain or the type of home in which they live, and so on.

4. In the box below the question "How are they alike?" have students write four ways in which the setting from the book is similar to the setting in which they live.

5. In the boxes below the question "How are they different?" students can list four ways in which the settings differ. They might consider various criteria such as climate, landscape, economy, location, flora, fauna, population, culture, history, and politics. Have them write the criteria they're using for each comparison above the bidirectional arrows.

Teacher Tip

This graphic organizer can also be used to compare and contrast other literary elements. Students can compare one character with another or with themselves, similar problems that characters from two different novels faced, the protagonist with the antagonist, and so on. When reading nonfiction, students can compare animal species or habitats, historical figures, cultures, regions or landforms, and so on.

Name _____ Date _____

There's No Place Like Home

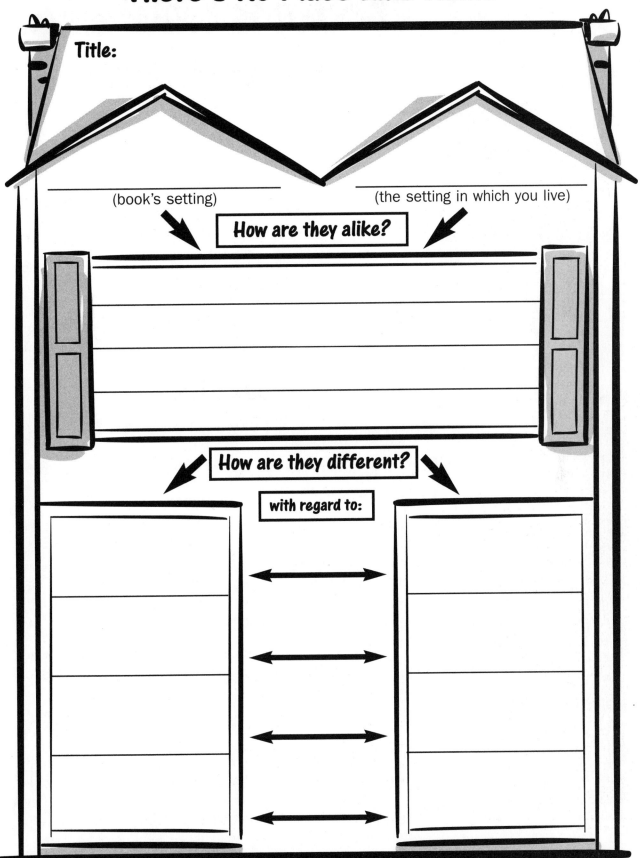

Title:

(book's setting)

(the setting in which you live)

How are they alike?

How are they different?

with regard to:

The Good, the Bad, and the Ugly

Materials

- 12- by 18-inch sheets of white card stock or oaktag
- scissors
- colored construction paper
- colored markers or pencils

Purpose

Students will examine similarities and differences between the protagonist and the antagonist in a story they are reading.

Directions

1. Cut sheets of 12- by 18-inch white card stock or oaktag in half vertically. Give one half sheet to each student.

2. Ask students to fold their sheet of paper in half as shown.

3. Have students draw an outline of a human figure on the folded sheet of paper. The figure's hands should be raised.

4. Show students how to cut out the figure's outline, cutting through both sides of the paper, and making sure not to sever the two halves. The figure's hands should remain connected.

5. Let students use markers and construction paper to dress one side like the protagonist and the opposite side like the antagonist.

6. Ask students to write information about each of the characters (traits, conflicts, actions, and so on) on the underside.

7. Display the characters on a table or shelf.

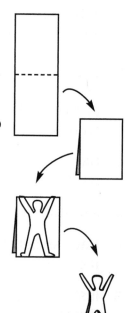

Cross-Curriculum

Students can compare opposing views of historical conflicts. An American colonist and King George III could debate the issue of taxation without representation. A Northerner and a Southerner could examine the issues that led to the Civil War.

Envelope Books

Materials

- 8½- by 11-inch sheets of copier paper
- #10 envelopes
- rulers
- scissors
- glue sticks
- colored markers and pencils

Purpose

Students will analyze the ways in which events in a story impact a character's development.

Directions

The following directions are for a four-page envelope book. You can adapt them to make longer books.

1. Before your class starts reading a novel, choose four major milestones in the plot—moments where a character goes through a life-changing event, has an epiphany, or overcomes an obstacle.

2. Give each student four envelopes and a sheet of white copier paper.

3. Ask students to cut a strip of paper that is 6 inches by 4 inches.

4. Have students place five tick marks at 1-inch intervals along the strip's length.

5. Instruct students to fan-fold the strip, using the tick marks as guides.

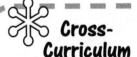

Cross-Curriculum

Help students learn about first-person reporting by having them write letters in the voice of a soldier writing home from the battlefield of a historic war. The letters can trace the progression of the war—the reasons it began, its major milestones, and its outcome.

6. Instruct students to lay the strip on their desk so the side with three peaks is face up. Have students put some glue in the two valleys and stick them together. They will now have four flaps radiating from the spine of the binding.

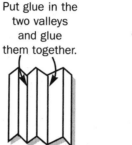

Put glue in the two valleys and glue them together.

This will create a spine with four flaps.

7. Have students put glue on the back of the first flap and stick it to the front left edge of the first envelope.

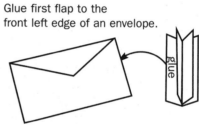

Glue first flap to the front left edge of an envelope.

8. Have students put glue on the back of the second flap and stick it to the front left edge of the second envelope. They can do the same with the third and fourth envelopes. Students now have a book whose pages are envelopes into which they can insert letters and other information.

9. As the class reads the novel, stop at four points in the book and ask students to write a letter from the point of view of the main character, addressing things the character has done, what he or she has learned, and how he or she feels at this point in the story. The letter can address problems the character faces and ways they might be solved, or it can delve into his or her relationships with other characters. The letter can be written to any other character in the book.

10. Have students insert the letter into the appropriate envelope and create an address for the character to whom it is being sent. Encourage students to design a stamp that reflects the contents of the letter, the setting of the story, or a plot element.

Teacher Tip

Give students a chance to develop their visual arts skills by having them draw pictures to accompany each letter. Or have them create a postcard to insert into each envelope; the postcard can feature a picture on the front and writing on the back.

Real-Life Character Cubes

Materials

- CHARACTER CUBE templates (pages 74 and 75)
- colored markers and pencils
- scissors
- glue sticks

Purpose

Students will analyze the character traits of a real-life person they're studying and make connections between this person's life and people or events in their own lives.

Directions

1. Pass out copies of the two CHARACTER CUBE templates to each student. (For sturdier cubes, copy the templates onto card stock.)

2. Ask students to follow the directions to fill out each of the panels.

3. Tell them to cut out the cube pieces along the solid lines.

4. Instruct them to glue tab A behind the bottom of Panel 4.

5. Show students how to fold the paper along the dotted lines so it forms a cube.

6. Have students glue each of the tabs behind the panel it meets.

Teacher Tip

Create a mobile of students' character cubes so viewers can see all six sides. Hang a string across the classroom. Tie threads of varying lengths along the string. Tie a paper clip to the end of each piece of thread. Fasten the character cubes to the paper clips so they create a long mobile of students' work.

Character Cube Template 1

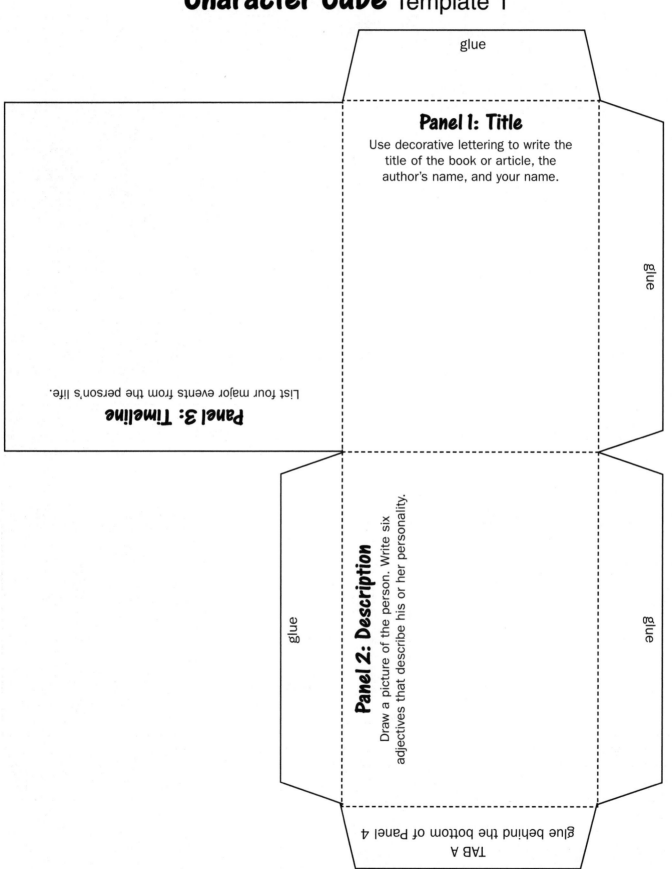

glue

Panel 1: Title
Use decorative lettering to write the title of the book or article, the author's name, and your name.

glue

Panel 3: Timeline
List four major events from the person's life.

glue

Panel 2: Description
Draw a picture of the person. Write six adjectives that describe his or her personality.

glue

TAB A
glue behind the bottom of Panel 4

Character Cube Template 2

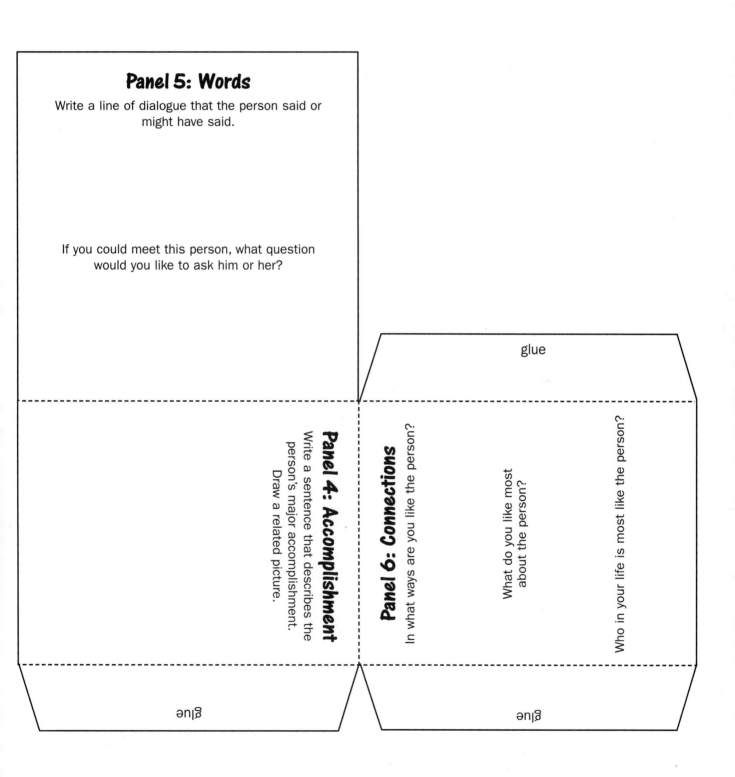

Panel 5: Words

Write a line of dialogue that the person said or might have said.

If you could meet this person, what question would you like to ask him or her?

glue

Panel 4: Accomplishment

Write a sentence that describes the person's major accomplishment. Draw a related picture.

Panel 6: Connections

In what ways are you like the person?

What do you like most about the person?

Who in your life is most like the person?

glue

glue

Looking at Dialogue

Say What?

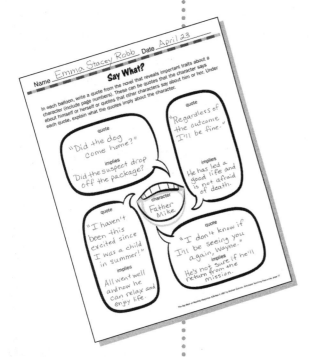

Purpose

Students will examine how dialogue reveals character.

Directions

1. Pass out a copy of the SAY WHAT? graphic organizer to each student.

2. As students read a novel, ask them to look for passages of dialogue that reveal information about someone's character. The dialogue might reveal something about the speaker, or it might reveal something about another character in the novel. See if students can find four passages spoken by the same character.

3. Have students write the speaker's name in the center of the SAY WHAT? graphic organizer. Then have them write a quote in each of the speech balloons, along with the page number where the dialogue was found.

4. Beneath each quote, have students write what the dialogue reveals about another character or the speaker himself or herself.

Teacher Tip

Find examples of dialogue in stories that reinforce the adage "You can't always believe what you hear." Remind students that just because a character says something does not mean it's true. Often, untrue statements that a character makes can reveal as much as or more than factual statements. They can reveal insecurities, jealousies, ignorance, intolerance, a sense of humor, and so on.

Say What?

In each speech balloon, write one or more lines of dialogue from the novel that reveal something important about a character. The dialogue might reveal something about the speaker himself or herself, or it might reveal something about another character. Beneath each quote, explain what the dialogue implies about the character. Be sure to include the page number where the dialogue was found.

(Title of Book) _____

quote

implies

quote

implies

quote

implies

character

quote

implies

A Story's Voice

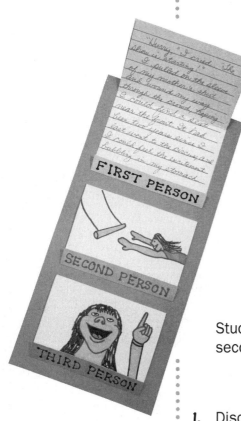

First, Second, and Third

Materials

- FIRST, SECOND, AND THIRD writing template (page 80)
- scissors
- colored markers and pencils
- 12- by 18-inch sheets of construction paper
- glue sticks

Purpose

Students will differentiate stories written in the first, second, and third person.

Directions

1. Discuss the concept of voice in a story and how stories can be written in first, second, or third person.

2. Read the following three paragraphs to the class:

   First Person—"Hurry," I cried. "The show is starting!" I pulled on the sleeve of my mother's shirt and wound my way through the crowd, hoping I could find a seat near the front.

   Second Person—It had been two years since you last went to a circus. You could feel the excitement bubbling in your stomach as the acrobats jumped onto the trapeze thirty feet above your head.

   Third Person—Pooja's grin stretched from ear to ear as she watched the aerial display. Her head was cocked at an uncomfortable angle. Because there were three rings, she had to constantly shift her gaze so that she wouldn't miss a single thing.

3. Give each student two copies of the FIRST, SECOND, AND THIRD writing template.

Teacher Tip

Use this activity to help students understand past, present, and future tense. Have students write three paragraphs to examine a topic from three different perspectives. For example, they could write about what they learned last year in school, what they're working on in the current school year, and what they hope to accomplish next year.

4. Have students cut the pages in half along the dotted line. Each student will need three halves. They can reserve the fourth half as a backup in case they make a mistake.

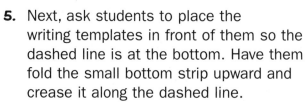

5. Next, ask students to place the writing templates in front of them so the dashed line is at the bottom. Have them fold the small bottom strip upward and crease it along the dashed line.

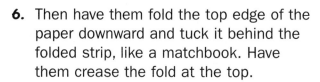

6. Then have them fold the top edge of the paper downward and tuck it behind the folded strip, like a matchbook. Have them crease the fold at the top.

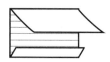

7. Have them repeat these steps for the other two sheets.

8. Across the lower front strips of the three "matchbooks" instruct students to write "First Person," "Second Person," and "Third Person."

9. Choose three paragraphs from a novel that the students are reading, and tell students to rewrite the paragraphs on the inside of the matchbooks, changing the voice accordingly. Have students read the first paragraph and rewrite it in the first person, read the second paragraph and rewrite it in the second person, and read the third paragraph and rewrite it in the third person. (In all likelihood the paragraphs you choose will be written in either the first or third person, so in one of the matchbooks, students won't be changing the point of view.)

10. Have students close their matchbooks and draw a picture on the cover of each that expresses the main idea of the paragraph inside.

11. Give each student a sheet of construction paper. Have students cut their sheet into a 7- by 14-inch rectangle. Ask them to glue their three paragraphs onto the construction paper (see photo on page 78).

12. Ask students to discuss reasons the author might have written the story in the voice he or she chose. Encourage students to examine how the story would have changed if it had been told in a different voice.

Teacher Tip

The most frequently used voices in writing are first and third. First person has the advantage of being very personal. The reader knows exactly what the storyteller feels or does. However, this also presents limitations. The story can't jump from character to character or location to location; it must remain in the same location as the narrator. We cannot know or witness anything the narrator does not tell us. Third person, or omniscient voice, is probably the easiest voice to use. It allows the author to tell the reader anything, from any character's point of view or from any location. In essence, the narrator sounds like the author. Second person is rarely used in fiction. The constant use of *you, you, you* prevents the reader from identifying with or empathizing with any of the characters.

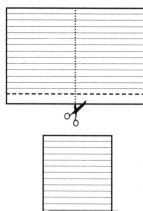

That's Life

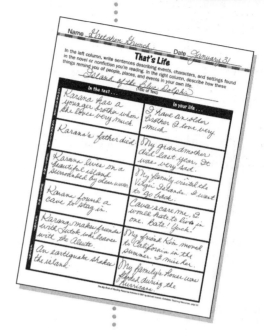

Materials

– THAT'S LIFE graphic organizer (page 82)

Purpose

Students will make connections between characters or simple events in a novel or informational text and people or events in their own life.

Directions

1. Pass out copies of the THAT'S LIFE graphic organizer to students.

2. Ask students to write sentences in the left column describing events, settings, and characters in a story they're reading.

3. In the right column, students write ways in which these things remind them of people, places, and events in their own lives. They can begin these sentences with phrases such as "This reminds me of . . ." or "This is like . . ."

4. Ask students to discuss these similarities in small groups or as a whole class. Encourage them to make connections between the text and other texts they have read, occurrences in their own lives, and events throughout the world.

Book Talk

"Connecting to text helps readers:
• understand how characters feel and the motivation behind their actions.
• have a clearer picture in their head thus making them more engaged.
• set a purpose for reading and keeps them focused.
• see how other readers connected to the reading.
• remember what they have read and ask questions about the text."
   —Cris Tovani,
I Read It, But I Don't Get It: Comprehension Strategies for Adolescent Readers, Stenhouse, 2000.

Name _____ Date _____

That's Life

In the left column, write sentences describing events, characters, and settings found in the novel or nonfiction you're reading. In the right column, describe how these things remind you of people, places, and events in your own life.

_____
(Title of Text)

	In the text . . .	In your life . . .
CHARACTER		
CHARACTER		
SETTING		
SETTING		
EVENT		
EVENT		

Figuratively Speaking

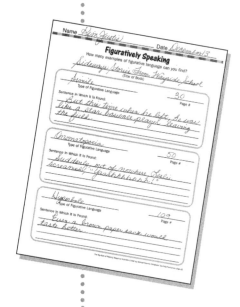

Materials

- FIGURATIVE LANGUAGE reproducible (page 84)
- FIGURATIVELY SPEAKING graphic organizer (page 85)

Purpose

Students will explore ways in which figurative language is used in literary texts.

Directions

1. Pass out copies of the FIGURATIVE LANGUAGE reproducible and discuss the meanings of the different figures of speech. You might want to focus on a few specific types, rather than on all of them at once.

2. Once students understand the different figures of speech, pass out copies of the FIGURATIVELY SPEAKING graphic organizer for students to fill out as they read a story or novel.

3. Ask students to look for examples of figurative language in a book they're reading. They should write the name of the type of figurative language they found and the page number they found it on. Below that they should write the full sentence in which it appears and circle or highlight the figurative phrase.

Teacher Tip

Encourage students to develop an ear for figurative language. As you conduct a read-aloud, invite students to raise their hand whenever they hear an example. Ask them to identify the figure of speech they heard. If they're correct, give them a small ticket or coupon. Have them write their name on the ticket and place it in a jar on your desk. After finishing the novel, draw a name and reward the winner in some way. The more examples a student finds in a read-aloud, the more chances he or she has to win!

Name _____ Date _____

Figurative Language

Idiom

*an expression whose meaning is different from the ordinary meaning
of the words*

Example: John *let the cat out of the bag* when he accidentally
told Jane about the surprise party.

Simile

*a figure of speech in which two dissimilar things are compared
by the use of <u>like</u> or <u>as</u>*

Example: The fog hugged the mountain like a warm coat.

Metaphor

*a figure of speech in which two dissimilar things are compared
without using the words <u>like</u> or <u>as</u>*

Example: The clouds were a wagon train lumbering across the
January sky.

Onomatopoeia

the use of a word whose spoken sound suggests the actual sound

Example: *Whoosh!* the winds cried loudly. *Rumble!* the clouds
thundered in reply.

Hyperbole

an extreme exaggeration, often used for comic effect

Example: "I've told you a thousand times to
settle down," the man told his children.

Personification

to show something that is not human behaving in a human or lifelike way

Example: The mountain became king, standing proudly in his royal
white robes of snow, surveying the realm around him.

Figuratively Speaking

How many examples of figurative language can you find?

_____

(Title of Book)

_____   _____

Type of figurative language   Page #

Sentence in which it is found:

_____

_____

_____

_____

_____   _____

Type of figurative language   Page #

Sentence in which it is found:

_____

_____

_____

_____

_____   _____

Type of figurative language   Page #

Sentence in which it is found:

_____

_____

_____

_____

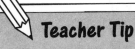

Improving
Vocabulary

Vocabulary Robots

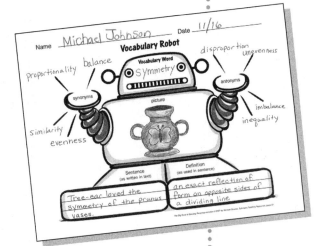

Purpose

Students will learn the meanings of new vocabulary words found in fiction or informational texts they are reading.

Directions

1. Pass out copies of the VOCABULARY ROBOT graphic organizer to students.

2. Ask students to write a vocabulary word from a novel, textbook, or article they are reading. They should write the word inside the robot's head.

3. Have them write the sentence containing the vocabulary word on the robot's left boot.

4. Have students find the definition for the word as it is used in the sentence and write that definition on the right boot.

5. Invite students to use a thesaurus to find four synonyms and four antonyms for the word and write them on the robot's hands.

6. Finally, have students draw a picture of the word on the robot's body. If the word is not a concrete noun, they may need to illustrate the concept (especially if the word is a feeling, an adjective, or an idea).

Teacher Tip

Copy the VOCABULARY ROBOT graphic organizer on both sides of three-hole copier paper so students can create a vocabulary journal. Encourage them to use a three-ring binder or pocket folder to store all the vocabulary words they learn throughout the year.

Name _____

Date _____

Vocabulary Robot

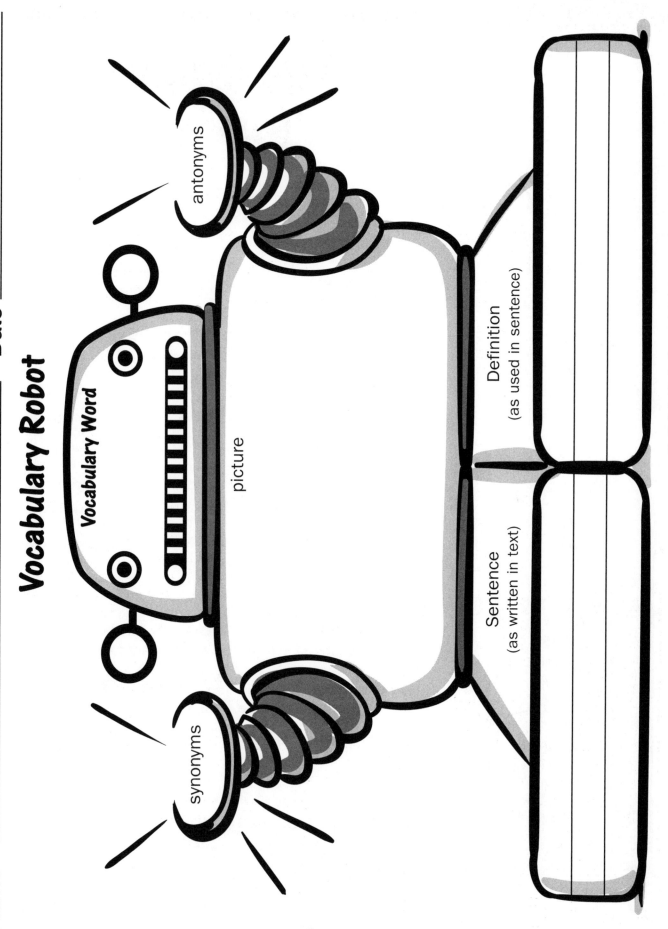

antonyms

Vocabulary Word

synonyms

picture

Sentence
(as written in text)

Definition
(as used in sentence)

Cause and Effect

The Ripple Effect

Materials

- THE RIPPLE EFFECT graphic organizer (page 89)

Purpose

Students will analyze the ways in which an action can have multiple repercussions.

Directions

1. Discuss the idea that when you throw a stone into water, the ripple spreads in all directions and can have an effect on several different things. A duck might take flight because of the sound, a boat might rock because of the wave, a sandy beach might erode when the wave hits the shore, and a fish might dodge the descending stone. And each of these effects might in turn create further repercussions.

2. Relate this concept to an occurrence in a novel or nonfiction text that students are reading. An author might create a situation in which an action affects other events and characters in the story; a single political act might have resounding repercussions (for example, the Tea Tax during the American Revolution led to the Boston Tea Party, which in turn led to the Intolerable Acts).

3. Pass out copies of THE RIPPLE EFFECT graphic organizer to students, and ask them to write a sentence describing an action (by a character, real-life individual, political body, or nature) from a novel or nonfiction text they are reading.

4. As the students continue reading, have them write down the many different effects that result from this single action. If these effects cause further repercussions in the story or text, have students list these, too.

Teacher Tip

As a creative-writing exercise, ask students to write a cause-and-effect story. You might provide a cause, such as "Mr. Smith forgot to set his alarm clock" or "Mrs. Jones dropped her wallet," and have students use that scenario as a starting point. Then ask volunteers to read their stories. Discuss how the same cause resulted in different outcomes.

The Ripple Effect

Write the cause on the boat
and its effects on each ripple.

CAUSE

EFFECTS

3, 2, 1, Blastoff!

Materials

- 3, 2, 1, BLASTOFF! graphic organizer (page 91)

Purpose

Students will identify what they learned and what they still want to know after reading an informational text.

Directions

1. Give each student a copy of the 3, 2, 1, BLASTOFF! graphic organizer.

2. As students read a textbook or nonfiction article, have them record three things they learned, two things they found interesting, and one question they still have after reading the selection.

3. Ask students to share and discuss their findings in small groups or as a whole class.

Teacher Tip

While this graphic organizer lends itself to discussing textbooks, it can be used as a way for students to respond to any type of book, including fiction.

3, 2, 1, Blastoff!

3 things I learned

2 things I found interesting

1 question I still have

Here's How I See It

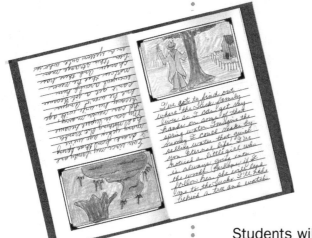

Materials

- HERE'S HOW I SEE IT template (page 93)
- stapler
- colored markers and pencils
- 9- by 12-inch construction paper

Purpose

Students will develop an understanding of the importance of point of view in a fiction or nonfiction text.

Directions

1. Discuss the idea that a story takes on a very different slant depending on who is telling it. Ask students to suggest situations where this might be the case, such as a legal dispute, a war, or a fight between a superhero and a villain. Even a wedding, a party, or a vacation could be experienced very differently by two individuals.

2. Make double-sided copies of the HERE'S HOW I SEE It template.

3. Give each student several two-sided copies of the template and a sheet of light-colored construction paper. Ask students to stack the pages and fold them in half (like the pages of a book). The construction paper will serve as the cover of the book. Staple the pages along the spine. When the book is opened, the right-hand pages will face one way and the left-hand pages the other.

4. Have students read a selection from a novel, textbook, or nonfiction article and use the "upside-down books" to write about the situation from the points of view of two different characters or participants. Ask students to design a cover, open the book, and use the right-hand pages for the first story. They can write the story on the lines and use the snapshots to illustrate it. Then have students flip the book over, design a new cover, and use the new right-hand pages for the second story.

✲ Cross-Curriculum

No country goes to war without a lot of agonized consideration. They don't spend money and risk lives unless they think they are in the right. Therefore it is always interesting and educational to look at historic battles. Have students create upside-down books to explore these conflicts from the points of view of both sides.

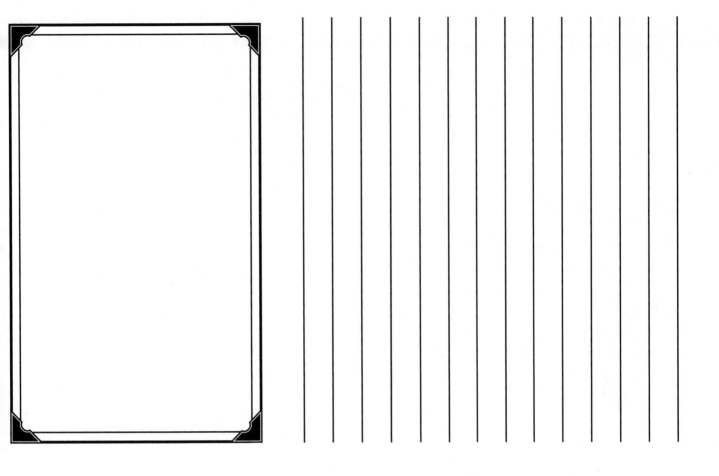

Here's How I See It Template

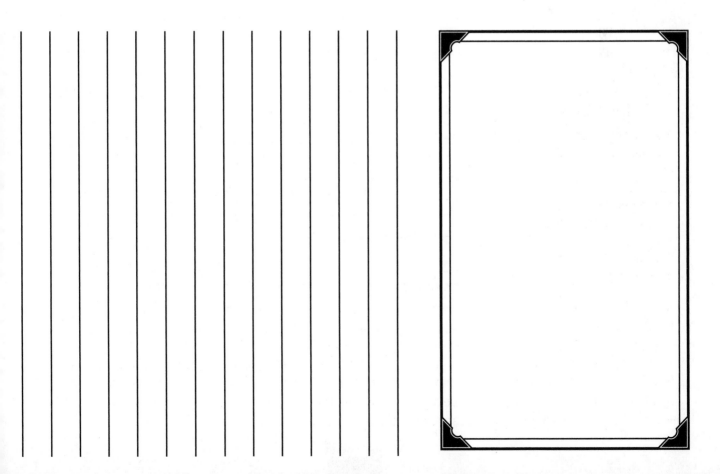

Rising and Falling Action

Ups and Downs

Materials

- RISING AND FALLING ACTION graphic organizer (page 95)

Purpose

Students will analyze the way in which a story builds toward a climax and resolution.

Directions

1. Discuss with the class the idea of rising and falling action— how a story builds over time, leading to a climax and then quickly concludes. Use a familiar story, such as *The Wizard of Oz* or *Charlotte's Web*, to point out these elements. (For example, here are a few of the many obstacles in *The Wizard of Oz*: Miss Gulch takes Toto, a tornado comes, Dorothy is trapped in Oz, and Dorothy goes through the haunted forest. These all lead to the climactic confrontation between Dorothy and the Wicked Witch of the West.)

2. Give each student a copy of the RISING AND FALLING ACTION graphic organizer.

3. As students read a novel, ask them to write ten simple phrases or sentences that describe events and obstacles that happen in the story.

4. When they get to the climax, have students write a sentence or phrase describing it in the box at the top of the mountain.

5. After students finish the novel, ask them to list four phrases that describe events that are part of the falling action.

6. Finally, ask students to write phrases that summarize the major problem and solution of the story in the box at the bottom of the page.

Teacher Tip

Use this graphic organizer as a starting point for a class-made bulletin board that focuses on rising and falling action. Explain to students that most novels contain a series of obstacles that the protagonist must overcome. Have students create a series of ever-increasing mountains out of brown bulletin board paper. The size of the mountain is determined by the scope of the problem. The tallest mountain should be the one that represents the climax. Students can draw a picture and write a paragraph on each mountain explaining the obstacle or event leading up to the climax. Have students rumple the paper to mimic the mountain's terrain. They can add snowcapped peaks to the taller mountains. To add a finishing touch, have students create climbers, goats, clouds, trees, skiers, chalets, and so on.

Name _____   Date _____

Rising and Falling Action

Climax:

Falling Action

Rising Action

11.

12.

13.

14.

Problem:

Solution:

10.

9.

8.

7.

6.

5.

4.

3.

2.

1.

Literature Response

Chapter Scrapbooks

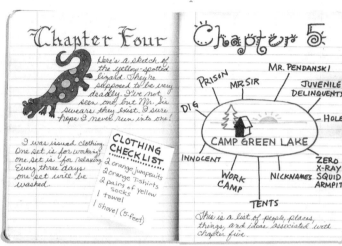

Materials

- SCRAPBOOK IDEAS reproducible (page 97)
- SCRAPBOOK SNAPSHOT template (page 98)
- composition notebooks
- various craft materials and paper
- colored markers and pencils

Purpose

Students will use reading and writing skills and strategies to respond to a work of fiction.

Directions

1. Ask each student to bring a composition notebook to class.

2. Pass out a copy of the SCRAPBOOK IDEAS reproducible to each student.

3. After students have read the first chapter in a novel, have them to use a double-page spread in the notebook to design a scrapbook entry for that chapter. The pages can feature a variety of information related to the chapter, a character, the setting, the events, and so on. Remind students to include a chapter number or name.

4. For ideas, students can refer to the SCRAPBOOK IDEAS handout or come up with their own ideas. Or you can assign specific things for each chapter that you want the students to feature on each page.

5. Have students create new scrapbook entries after they complete each chapter. At the end of the novel, students will have created a chapter-by-chapter scrapbook that you can collect for grading.

Teacher Tip

Students can create "point of view" scrapbooks where the left-hand page is created from the point of view of one character and the right-hand page by another character. Or they can create "double entry" scrapbooks where the left-hand page is created as if by a character from the novel and the right-hand page details the student's response to the content on the previous page or to the content of the chapter.

Scrapbook Ideas

- Write a journal entry from a character's point of view that describes the plot of the chapter. Include a brief description of the following: other characters, setting, major events, and conclusion.
- Write a letter from the character to an advice columnist that describes the major problem in the chapter. The columnist's response should suggest a possible solution.
- Create, draw, or collect souvenirs or mementos that the character would have put into the scrapbook. Include an explanation next to each object describing its significance.
- Write a diary entry from the character's point of view that reflects the character's feelings about himself or herself. Include ways in which the character changes over the course of the story.
- Use the SNAPSHOT template to create "photographs" that illustrate the character in a scene from the book, the character's major accomplishment, the setting of the story, and so on. Write a sentence or two next to the snapshot to explain it.
- Write about a character's typical day.
- Include a sketch of a hobby a character has.
- Create a newspaper article that includes the "5 Ws" of an event that happened in the chapter.
- Create a weather report that shows what the weather was like in the chapter. What does the main character like/dislike about the weather or the setting?
- Create a ticket stub for a movie, sporting event, or concert a character attended. Write a review.
- List five things the character is thankful for. Include an icon for each.
- Draw a scene of a climactic event that happened in the chapter. How did the main character feel about it?
- Glue a "family photo" of a character to the page. Write five adjectives that describe each person shown.
- Find a leaf from a tree that could be found in the setting of the story and make a rubbing of it on the page. Print out a picture of the tree from the Internet and include it. Write some interesting facts about the tree.
- Who is the character's idol? Why? Attach a list of his or her accomplishments.
- Attach a timeline that shows each year a character has been alive. For each year, write a sentence that highlights a major event.
- Draw a map of the setting. Include a key.
- Create a "Top Ten" list related to one of the characters. Write about the number-one selection.
- Create a graphic organizer that compares and contrasts this chapter and a previous one.
- Create a graphic organizer that compares the way a character felt and acted at the beginning of the story and at the end of the story.
- Draw a comic strip that highlights the main events that happened in the chapter.
- Write three interview questions you'd like to ask one of the characters. How do you think he or she would respond? Include the responses.
- Write words from the chapter that you find interesting or unfamiliar. Write their definitions.
- Copy a sentence from the chapter that you think is well written. Why do you like this sentence?
- Write down an important line spoken by the character? Explain its significance.

Scrapbook Snapshots Template

Life Lessons

Materials

- THE MORAL OF THE STORY template (page 100)
- various Aesop's Fables
- scissors

Purpose

Students will examine the ways in which a story's moral teaches a lesson.

Directions

1. Read a few of Aesop's Fables to the class. Discuss the morals of the stories.

2. Cut out the moral cards on THE MORAL OF THE STORY template. Use the blank cards to create additional ones of your own.

3. Divide the class into groups of four or five.

4. Give each group one of the morals. (Or you could have each group write its own moral, such as "If you don't brush your teeth, you'll get cavities," or "When you eat well, you feel better.")

5. Ask each group to create a two- or three-minute scene that illustrates the meaning of the moral. The students should not actually say the moral while performing the scene.

6. Encourage groups to not take the moral literally. For example, if the moral is "Don't put all your eggs in one basket," groups should not create a scene that includes eggs and baskets. Instead, they could create a scene in which someone applies to only one high school and is not accepted—a story which reflects the moral.

7. When each group finishes its presentation, ask the rest of the class to guess the moral.

8. Ask students if anyone can tell you the underlying theme of the fables and presentations. Offer prompts until someone states that the theme is "life lessons."

Teacher Tip

Remember not to confuse *theme* and *moral*. A moral is a specific lesson that a story teaches. A theme on the other hand is a unifying idea that is a recurrent element within a literary work or collection of works. Therefore, each of Aesop's fables has a moral, while the theme of all his works is "life lessons."

The Moral of the Story

Don't judge a book by its cover.

Don't put all your eggs in one basket.

You can catch more flies with honey than with vinegar.

Slow and steady wins the race.

Two wrongs don't make a right.

The early bird catches the worm.

Appearances can be deceiving.

Birds of a feather flock together.

Don't count your chickens before they hatch.

Persuasion is better than force.

Honesty is the best policy.

Don't believe everything you hear.

Look before you leap.

A bird in the hand is worth two in the bush.

A liar will not be believed even when he tells the truth.

Making Choices

Materials

- MAKING CHOICES templates (pages 103–104)
- sheets of colored paper
- scissors
- colored pencils and markers
- glue sticks
- string
- thread
- paper clips

Purpose

Students will examine the ways in which the choices a character makes affect the outcome of the story.

Directions

1. Copy template 1 onto colored paper. Give each student three copies of this template. Use different colors for each copy. This will make the final projects more colorful.

2. Copy template 2 on white paper. Give each student one copy.

3. Ask students to pick one of the major choices that the main character makes in a novel they've recently read. On a copy of template 1, have students write a complete, detailed paragraph describing the situation the character was in before making the choice, the choice he or she made, and the consequences of that choice.

4. On the copy of template 2, have students draw a picture of the main character carrying out the choice he or she has made.

5. Ask students to draw a line down the middle of their second copy of template 1. Have them label the left side "Alternate Choices" and the right side "Consequences." Then have them write the number 1 on the first line of both sides of the vertical line; they should write the number 2 on both sides, about ten lines down.

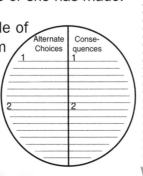

Teacher Tip

Discuss with the class the fact that all choices have consequences. Some consequences are positive, some are negative, and some have elements of both. Ask volunteers to describe a choice that they made and the consequences of that choice. Decide which category the conse-quences fall into. Discuss alternative choices that the student could have made and how the consequences would have been different.

6. Ask students to write two alternate choices that the main character could have made instead of the choice he or she did make. Beside each choice, tell students to list the consequences that would have resulted if that choice had been made. These consequences should be completely different from anything that actually happened in the story.

7. Ask students to select one of the two alternate choices/consequences from the previous step. On the last copy of template 1, ask them to write a new ending for the book, showing how this choice would have affected the outcome of the story.

8. After students have completed the four pages, ask them to cut out the circles.

9. Have students fold each of the circles in half vertically so the information is inside the fold.

10. Instruct students to glue the back right side of one circle to the back left side of a second circle.

11. Then have students glue the back right side of the second circle to the back left side of a third circle.

12. Have students repeat this for the third and fourth circles.

13. Finally, students should finish the circle book by gluing the right side of the fourth circle to the left side of the first circle.

14. Hang a string across your classroom. Tie varying lengths of thread from the string. Attach a paper clip to the end of each piece of thread and hang the circle books from the paper clips. When a breeze blows past the circle books, they will spin and create a vibrant display of the students' work.

Cross-Curriculum

Circle books can be made from any symmetrically cut piece of paper, such as suns, stars, triangles, and paper doll figures. Think of a shape that relates to your curriculum—cloud books for a unit on weather, heart books for the human body, or flower books for plant life.

102

Making Choices Template 1

Making Choices Template 2

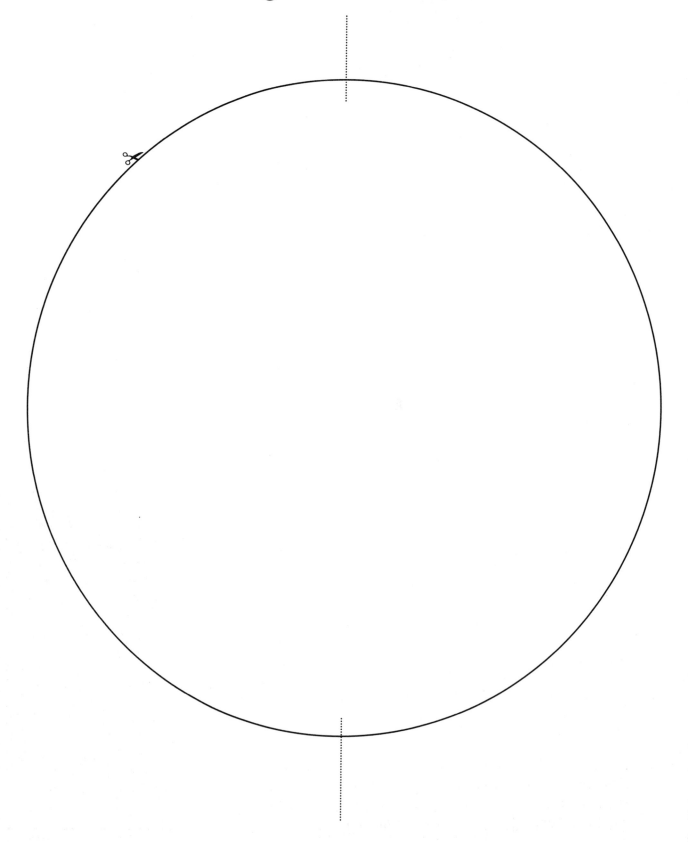

Radio Plays

Materials

- recordings of old radio shows
- writing paper
- tape recorder
- blank tapes
- construction paper
- colored pencils and markers
- plastic sandwich bag

Purpose

Students will work in cooperative groups to retell the story of a real-life event in the style of a radio newscast.

Directions

1. Before having your students work on this project, visit your local library and check out audiotapes of old radio shows, such as mysteries, westerns, newscasts, and comedies. Play portions of the tapes for the class and encourage students to listen to the ways characters and settings are described, the sound effects that are used, the background music and theme music that are used, and the way dialogue helps propel the story forward. Because radio is an aural medium—without the aid of visuals—dialogue is especially integral to the storytelling.

2. Compare the sound effects of a mystery with those of a western or comedy. Ask students to suggest ways the sound effects might have been made.

3. Divide the class into groups. Invite each group to write a radio play based on a historical or current event they've studied. Encourage them to use as much dialogue as possible to tell the story, keeping narration to a minimum.

Teacher Tip

Here are some ways to vary the activity: Have students create radio plays that focus on a specific genre or author; assign different chapters from a class novel for each group to adapt; invite students to create radio newscasts that detail the politics, trends, and events from different decades of the twentieth century.

This activity can tap into the many learning styles in your classroom. Interpersonal learners will benefit from the cooperative interaction of the group. Verbal/linguistic learners will excel at writing the script and storytelling. Aural learners will enjoy creating the audiotape and listening to the other groups' tapes. Kinesthetic learners will have fun creating the sound effects that help establish the mood of the story. And the musical/rhythmic learners can find the right background and theme music for the piece as well as use instruments to help create the sound effects.

4. Students can participate in the creation of the radio play in several ways—

> *Scribes*: write the script; transcribe the final draft
> *Artists*: illustrate the script's cover; create the bulletin board design
> *Actors*: read the script; create unique characters using vocal expression
> *Technicians*: operate the tape recorder; hold the microphone; edit the recording
> *Musicians*: find the theme music; play instruments to create background music
> *Sound Designers*: find sound-effect materials; create the sound effects

Allow students to perform multiple jobs, so every member can help create the sound effects, assist in the writing of the script, and act in the radio play.

5. After the groups have finished writing their scripts, have them find background and theme music. Ask them to discuss the sound effects that their story needs. Challenge them to find ways to create those sounds, such as shaking rain sticks or boxes filled with pebbles, rattling cookie sheets, clapping wood blocks, crumpling paper, and so on.

6. Invite the groups to record their radio shows. Then let the rest of the class listen to the recordings.

7. Encourage groups to create a folio for their script with a cover illustration. Hang the scripts on a bulletin board, with the recording of the show in a plastic resealable bag underneath them. Invite teachers of younger grades to use the radio plays in their listening centers.

Documentary Film Scrolls

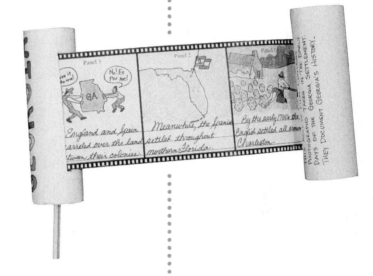

Materials

- tubes from paper towel rolls
- scissors
- rulers
- white construction paper
- tape
- FILMSTRIPS template (page 108)
- glue sticks
- colored markers and pencils
- drinking straws

Purpose

Students will sequence the key events of a historical period or in the life of a notable personality.

Directions

1. Ask students to bring in enough cardboard tubes from paper towel rolls so that each student has his or her own tube.

2. Have students cut their tube in half.

3. Instruct students to cover each of their tubes with white construction paper. Have them cut the construction paper so it extends a half inch beyond the ends. Then have students cut several slits in these overhanging edges so they can fold the edges inside the tubes. Have students tape the ends of the paper to the inside of the tubes.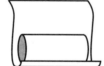

4. Ask students to cut a 4- by $1/4$-inch slot down the center of one of their tubes. (You may want to cut the slots yourself using a craft knife.)

5. Give each student a copy of the FILMSTRIP template and have them cut out the frames.

Teacher Tip

As an alternative activity, students can create a film scroll of photos that might have been taken by a secondary character over the course of a novel. The sentences accompanying each picture can be written from the point of view of this character and can explain why these pictures were taken.

6. Tell students to glue tab A on filmstrip 2 behind panel 3 on filmstrip 1.

7. Instruct students to choose six key scenes to illustrate from a biography or nonfiction book or article they've read. (Demonstrate how to draw the scenes on the filmstrip in chronological order from right to left, starting with panel 1.) Have students add a descriptive sentence to each frame that explains the scene's importance.

8. Ask students to bend the right-hand tab of their filmstrip backward and tape it to the tube that does not have the slot. (See illustration below.)

9. Next have them put a couple of pieces of tape on the left-hand tab and thread it through the slot in the second tube. Have them tape this tab to a straw that has been inserted into the roll. The straw will act as a lock, preventing the filmstrip from being pulled out of the slot. Students can trim the straw so that only a half inch of straw sticks out from each side of the tube.

10. Show students how to twist the straw, pulling the filmstrip into the left-hand tube. This will pull the two paper tubes together.

11. Have students write a title for their filmstrip on the left-hand tube and their name on the right-hand tube.

12. Demonstrate how the right-hand tube can be pulled to reveal the six scenes, chronologically, one panel at a time.

Cross-Curriculum

Ask students to create film scrolls that sequence the steps in a science experiment, highlight the parts of speech, or illustrate events that lead to the Civil War.

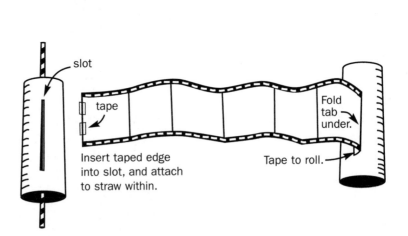

slot

tape

Insert taped edge into slot, and attach to straw within.

Fold tab under.

Tape to roll.

Filmstrips Template

Filmstrip 1

Filmstrip 2

Panel 3

Panel 6

Panel 2

Panel 5

Panel 1

Panel 4

Tape this tab to the right-hand tube.

TAB A: Glue this tab behind panel 3 on Filmstrip 1.

The Big Book of Reading Response Activities © 2007 by Michael Gravois, Scholastic Teaching Resources, page 109

I Packed a Suitcase

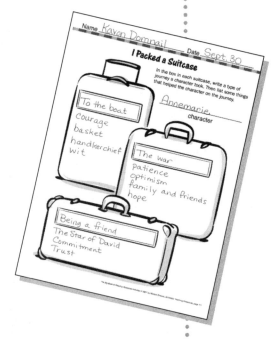

Materials

- I PACKED A SUITCASE graphic organizer (page 111)

Purpose

Students will examine the inner and outer journeys a character takes over the course of a novel.

Directions

1. Discuss the different kinds of journeys a character might take over the course of a novel—both literal and figurative. For example, in addition to an actual physical journey, a character can take an emotional, psychological, intellectual, moral, or spiritual journey.

2. Ask students to think about a novel they just finished reading and the types of journeys the main character took.

3. Give each student a copy of the I PACKED A SUITCASE graphic organizer.

4. In the rectangle on each suitcase, have students write a different type of journey the character took. Beneath the rectangle have them write a list of essential things that helped the character on the journey; these could be either actual objects from the story or symbolic concepts like courage, friendship, or faith.

Cross-Curriculum

In history or social studies class, have students complete a graphic organizer that lists items a tourist might pack for a trip to another country, a pioneer child might take on the journey west, or a time traveler might bring back from a voyage to another century.

I Packed a Suitcase

In the box in each suitcase, write a type of journey a character took. Then list some things that helped the character on the journey.

_____

character

Inner Life of Characters

Character Interviews

Materials

- sheets of white paper
- construction paper
- glue sticks
- scissors
- colored markers and pencils

Purpose

Students will explore the thoughts and feelings of a fictional character or real-life personality.

Directions

1. Give each student a sheet of white paper. The size can vary, but the larger the paper, the more writing space students will have.

2. Ask students to fold the paper into thirds as shown at right.

3. Have them fold it into thirds the other way.

4. Instruct students to open the paper and cut out the four corner pieces.

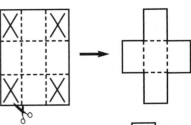

5. Have students fold the outer panels toward the center. The order doesn't matter.

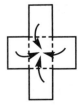

Cross-Curriculum

The four panels of the four-fold book lend themselves to reporting on topics that come in fours—four seasons (winter, spring, summer, fall), four elements (fire, water, earth, air), four major math functions (addition, subtraction, multiplication, division), and so on.

6. Tell students to select a fictional character or real-life individual from a novel or textbook they've just read.

7. On the top side of each of the four panels, have students write an interview question they would like to ask the character they selected. A list of sample questions appears below.

8. On the underside of each panel, have students write the character's response to the question posed on the top. Tell students to put themselves in the shoes of the character and to answer the question in the words they think the character would use.

9. Once the four panels are opened, it reveals a central panel. Have students draw a picture of the character they interviewed.

10. Have students use a glue stick to glue the back of the "four-fold book" to a sheet of construction paper. Have them write a title that includes the character's name, such as "An In-Depth Interview with Charlotte Doyle."

Sample Questions

- What was your childhood like?
- What is your relationship with your family members like?
- What are your hobbies?
- What is your greatest fear in life?
- Who is your best friend? Why?
- Who is your worst enemy? Why?
- What is the biggest problem you've ever faced?
- How did you overcome this problem?
- Where do you live? Do you like it?
- If you could live anywhere, where would it be?
- What is the most exciting thing that's ever happened to you?
- What is the worst thing that's ever happened to you?
- Who do you look up to the most?
- What kind of person annoys you?
- What is your typical day like?
- What are your best and worst traits?
- What makes you angry?
- What makes you happy?
- What do you dream about at night?

Teacher Tip

Students can write a four-fold "Mystery Book." Have students write the word "when" on the top panel. On the underside of the panel have them write a paragraph discussing the "when" of a certain thing or event. On the next three panels have them write the words "why," "where," and "who," and the corresponding paragraphs underneath. When the four flaps are lifted, the center panel is revealed. This panel can feature the word "what" with a description of the thing or event. Other students can see how many panels they have to lift before guessing the event at the center of the Mystery Book.

Story Maps

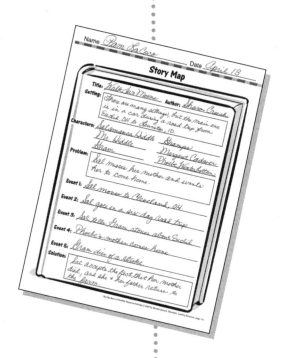

● ●

Materials

- STORY MAP graphic organizer (page 115)

Purpose

Students will demonstrate an understanding of basic story elements.

Directions

1. Pass out copies of the STORY MAP graphic organizer to students.

2. On the top lines, ask students to write the title and author of a book they've just completed.

3. Have students write a few sentences about the setting (or a list of adjectives that describe the setting or nouns that can be found in the setting).

4. Ask students to write the names of the major and minor characters on the appropriate lines.

5. Finally, have them write a couple of sentences describing the major problem in the story, five sentences that describe five major events that happened in the main body of the story, and a couple of sentences describing the solution to the problem.

Teacher Tip

One of the advantages of graphic organizers is that they usually provide a small amount of space for students to respond. This forces students to distill information down to its most essential elements and helps them state main ideas succinctly.

Name _____ Date _____

Story Map

Title: _____ Author: _____

Setting:

Characters: _____   _____

_____   _____

Problem:

Event 1: _____

Event 2: _____

Event 3: _____

Event 4: _____

Event 5: _____

Solution:

Living Pictures

Materials

- bulletin board paper
- various craft materials
- scissors
- glue
- tape

Purpose

Students will work in reading groups to summarize the main events from novels they've read.

Directions

1. Divide the class into reading groups that contain five or six students, and assign a different novel for each group to read.

2. After the students have finished reading the novels, ask them to meet in their reading groups to brainstorm a list of major events from the story. Have the groups choose the five most important events and create five "living pictures," or "frozen" scenes, to represent them. The students will freeze in position as if a picture had been taken of the event.

3. Encourage the students to use bulletin board paper and craft materials (such as paper bags, costume jewelry, fabric, masks, paper hats, and so on) to create a background and simple costumes to enhance the living pictures.

4. One student should act as a narrator, describing what is occurring in each scene. (A different student can narrate each scene.)

5. Invite the groups to set up their backgrounds, dress in their costumes, and present their living pictures to the rest of the class.

Teacher Tip

This activity exposes the class to the plots of several different novels. You can select novels by the same author, of a similar genre, or with a common theme. It also provides a wonderful opportunity for students to interact socially, discuss books, and decipher the main ideas of the story.

The Write Stuff

Materials

- LEARNING POSTER REQUIREMENT SHEET (page 119)
- BOOK REVIEW template (page 120)
- SNAPSHOTS template (page 121)
- copies of book sets by various authors
- Internet access
- 4-foot strips of bulletin board paper
- construction paper
- colored markers and pencils
- scissors
- glue sticks
- staplers

Purpose

Students will work in reading groups to create a poster that features information about the work, life, and accomplishments of an award-winning author.

Directions

1. Divide the class into groups and tell them that each group will create a learning poster that focuses on a different award-winning author, such as Katherine Paterson, Louis Sachar, Karen Cushman, and Avi. You can assign the authors to each group or you can allow groups to choose their own, but each author should have written several books.

2. Have each student in a group read a different novel by the same author.

3. Give each student a copy of the REQUIREMENT SHEET and review it with the class. Tell students that it will be up to each group to decide which group member will be responsible for completing each element of the learning poster. Stress that part of their final grade will be determined by how well they share in the production of the final poster. Tell them that all group members should proofread everything on the poster, regardless of who created each element. Spelling will count as part of their final grade.

Cross-Curriculum

Adapt the requirement sheet to fit biographical studies from any curricular area. Students can work in cooperative groups to create learning posters about explorers, artists, mathematicians, scientists, athletes, musicians, politicians, and so on.

4. Give each group a 4-foot section of bulletin board paper to use as the background of their learning poster. Using a different color for each group will create a more colorful display.

5. Pass out two copies of the SNAPSHOT template to each group and two copies of the BOOK REVIEW template to each student. Use the instructions below to guide the students in the construction of their book reviews.

6. As students create each section of the learning poster, they can attach it to the background.

7. After the learning posters are completed, hang them up in the hall so other classes can learn about these award-winning authors.

How to Construct the Book Reviews

1. Have students follow the directions on the requirement sheet to fill out the book review panels. After they've completed the four panels (two drawing templates and two writing templates), have them cut out the panels.

2. Have students fold each of the panels in half so the information is inside the fold.

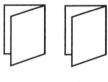

3. Instruct students to glue the back right side of the title panel (panel 1) to the back left side of the first writing template (panel 2).

4. Have students glue the back right side of panel 2 to the back left side of the second writing template (panel 3).

5. Then have students glue the back right side of panel 3 to the back left side of the panel with the drawing of the main character (panel 4).

6. Finally, students should put glue on the back right side of panel 4 to the back left side of panel 1 and attach the reviews to their learning poster.

Teacher Tip

Students can create longer book reviews by using more writing or drawing templates. Let them use as many as they need. Just have them attach the first and last panels to the poster as described in the directions at the right.

The Write Stuff Learning Poster
Requirement Sheet

☐ **Title**

Write the name of the author in large, decorative lettering across the top of your poster. List the names of each group member beneath the title.

☐ **Web Pages**

Do an online search to learn more about the author. Visit Web sites that feature biographical information, interviews, facts about his or her books, and so on. Print out several of the most informative pages. Highlight data that you find most interesting. Staple the pages together and attach them to your poster under the title "Web Search."

☐ **Timeline**

Create a timeline that features important events from the author's life as well as the publishing dates for his or her major books. Attach the timeline to your poster under the title "Timeline."

☐ **Snapshots**

Use three of the SNAPSHOTS templates to write paragraphs about interesting things that you learned about the author (his or her life, writing style, hobbies or interests, and so on) or the books you read (the themes, inspirations, significance, and so on). Draw a picture to accompany each paragraph. Attach the snapshots to your poster under the title "Interesting Information."

☐ **Awards**

Draw a picture of an important award that the author received. Cut out the drawing. Place it over lined paper, and cut the paper into the shape of the award. Staple the drawing and the paper together. Write about the significance of the award, its history, and why you think the author received it. Attach the award to your poster under the title "Congratulations!"

☐ **Graphic Organizer**

Create a Venn diagram that compares and contrasts:
- two characters from the book or
- the story's setting with your own community or
- events from the story with things that have happened in real life or
- events from the author's life with your own.

Attach the Venn diagram to your poster under the title "Making a Connection."

☐ **Book Review**

Each person in the group should use at least two copies of the BOOK REVIEW template to write a review on the book he or she read. Use the two drawing templates to create a title page (that includes the book's title and a related illustration) and a drawing of the main character in a scene from the book. Use the two writing templates to write a few paragraphs that highlight what you liked most about the book. Follow your teacher's instructions to construct the reports. Attach them to your poster under the title "Book Reviews."

Book Review

Drawing Template

Writing Template

Snapshots

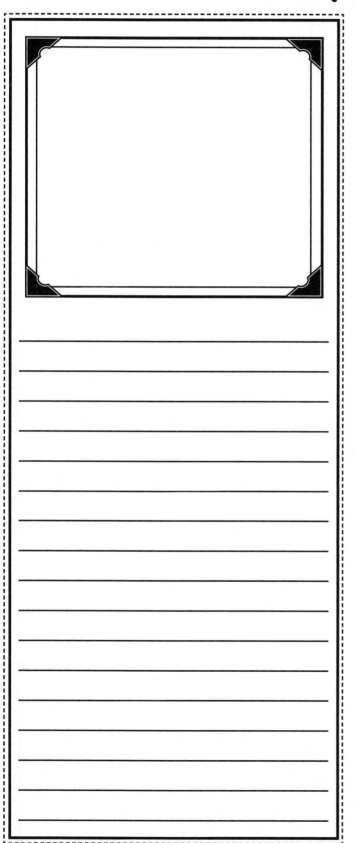

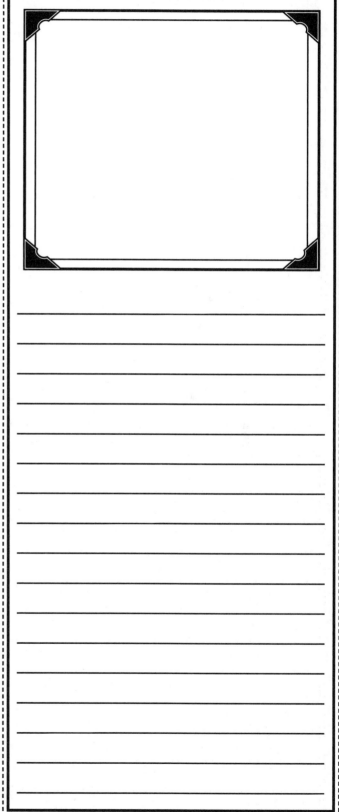

Buy the Book

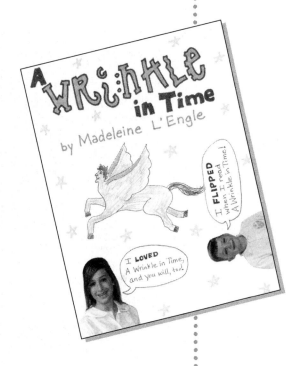

Materials

- magazines
- construction paper
- colored markers and pencils

Purpose

Students will use persuasive techniques to create advertisements for their favorite books.

Directions

1. Pass out copies of magazines and instruct students to examine the advertisements. Ask them to find examples of ways advertisers try to entice the readers into buying their products.

2. Review the following persuasive techniques found in advertising. Can your students find any examples of these techniques in the magazine ads?

Association—associating the product with fun times, patriotism, relaxation, or other desirable concepts

Bait and Switch—enticing consumers with a "free" offer when, in fact, the small print says they actually need four box tops, plus postage and handling

Bandwagon Technique—persuading people to buy a product by letting them know that other people are buying it

✳ Cross-Curriculum

Invite students to create advertisements that entice pioneers to move west, encourage classmates to exercise, challenge people to conserve energy, or persuade parents to get involved in the PTA.

Testimonials/Transfer—using the words (testimonials) or images (transfer) of famous people to persuade consumers to buy the product

Glittering Generalities—using exaggerated, flowery words to describe a product

Repetition—repeating the product's name at least four times to make you remember it

Statistics—quoting research, polls, or other numbers to help sell a product

3. Pass out large sheets of construction paper. Ask students to design a print ad for their favorite book that features one of the advertising techniques. (If you'd like to ensure that all the techniques are used, write the names of the various techniques on slips of paper. Invite the students to draw slips to determine the one they need to use in their advertisement.)

4. Allow students to use their own drawings, collage elements from magazines, tear art, watercolor, or any other artistic technique to create their ads.

Teacher Tip

For more detailed projects, ask students to work in cooperative groups to create a learning poster (similar to the one described in The Write Stuff on page 117) that uses several persuasive techniques to sell a favorite book. Groups can design print ads, write and record scripts for radio spots, compose a press release, or draw the storyboard for a television ad.

Beginning, Middle, and End

Jacob's Ladder Book

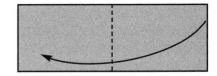
Purpose

Students will identify and describe the main idea of the beginning, middle, and end of a novel they've read.

Directions

A Jacob's Ladder Book can be made with any paper that is at least twice as long as it is wide. To aid in clarity, one side of the paper in this example is shown in gray and the other in white. Try making a sample before teaching this to your class. Creating these books takes a number of steps, but they're not difficult—and the end result is well worth the effort.

1. Pass out sheets of construction paper and have students cut them so they measure 8 inches by 18 inches.

2. Ask students to fold the paper in half.

3. Have students fold it in half a second time and then unfold it back one time.

4. Have them draw two lines from the folded edge to the center crease, $2\frac{1}{2}$ inches from the top and bottom edges of the paper. Then, have students cut along each of these lines.

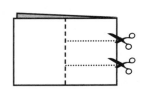

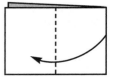

Teacher Tip

When leading a class through the construction of a complicated project like a Jacob's Ladder Book, it is important to make sure that every student completes each step before moving on to the next one. After carefully explaining each step, walk around the classroom to help students. Then make sure all eyes are on you before beginning the next step and that no student begins the task until you are finished giving the directions.

5. Ask students to open the paper completely and cut along the right edge of the flap.

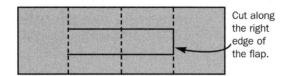

Cut along the right edge of the flap.

6. Instruct students to fold the center flap over to the left.

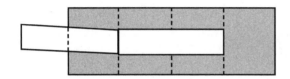

7. Ask students to fold the right page to the left.

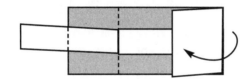

8. Tell them to fold it to the left a second time.

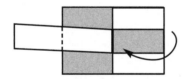

9. Instruct students to turn the book upside down, top to bottom. The flap will still be sticking out toward the left.

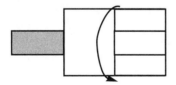

10. Ask students to fold the left flap over to the right and tape it to the right center flap. The tape will span the hole in the center of the book.

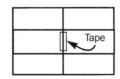

Tape

✳ Cross-Curriculum

Jacob's Ladder Books lend themselves to illustrating things that can be found in layers or at different levels; each page peels away to reveal the next layer. For example, pages 1 and 2 can feature information about the emergent and canopy layers of the rain forest, pages 3 and 4 the understory layer, and pages 5 and 6 the forest floor. Another book can be made about animals that live in the air, on land, and underwater. Or a book can illustrate the three layers of skin—the epidermis, dermis, and subcutaneous tissue.

11. Instruct students to close the book so the tape is on the outside spine of the cover. Ask them to press down on the edges of the book to make sharp creases.

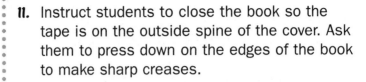
cover

12. Have students open the book to reveal pages 1 and 2. Tell students to mark the number 1 on the lower left panel of page 1 and the number 2 on the lower right panel of page 2.

13. Show students how to fold these pages backward so the cover panels meet in the back. The bottom panels of pages 1 and 2 will separate a little. Ask students to slip their thumbs into the gutter between pages 1 and 2 and open them to reveal pages 3 and 4. Have them mark these pages with the numbers 3 and 4.

14. Tell students to fold pages 3 and 4 backward, slip their thumbs into the gutter, and open them to reveal pages 5 and 6. Have them mark these pages with the numbers 5 and 6.

15. To close the book, students should reverse this process, pulling the pages together and then reaching to the back of the book to pull the next set of pages together.

16. Tell students to design a cover for their book that includes the title of the book they've read, an illustration, the author's name, and their own name.

17. Ask them to open the book to pages 1 and 2. As you see, each page is divided into three small panels. Tell students to write a paragraph across the bottom two panels that describes the main idea of the beginning of the story. Have students draw a related illustration in the upper area.

18. Tell students to open the book to pages 3 and 4 and write a paragraph across the bottom two panels that describes the main idea of the middle of the story. Have them draw a related illustration in the upper area.

19. Finally, instruct students to open the book to pages 5 and 6 and write a paragraph across the bottom two panels that describes the main idea of the end of the story. Have them draw a related illustration in the upper area.

Teacher Tip

Students can create Jacob's Ladder Books that contain vocabulary words, definitions, and sentences on each of the eighteen mini-panels within the book (three per page).

Lights! Camera! Action!

Materials

- copies of VIDEO CAMERA templates (pages 129–132)
- oaktag or posterboard
- scissors
- craft sticks
- tape
- stapler
- colored markers or pencils

Purpose

Students will illustrate and describe story elements from the point of view of a secondary character.

Directions

1. Discuss the way in which the events in a story might be interpreted differently by two particular characters. Tell students to imagine that a secondary character from a novel they've read held a video camera and recorded events and characters mentioned in the story—but as seen from their point of view. For example, Professor Snape might describe Hogwarts as an institution overrun with irritating school children; he might shoot a video of a Quidditch match and praise the performance of the Slytherin team; or he might aim the camera at that pesky little wizard with the lightning bolt-shaped scar and interrogate Harry Potter about his actions. Ask students to describe scenes that Hermione or Hagrid might have taken with a video camera.

2. Pass out copies of the FILM STRIPS and WRITING STRIPS templates on pages 131 and 132 to students.

✳ Cross-Curriculum

Video cameras can be used for countless activities. Students can take you on a microscopic journey through the human body, highlight major events and accomplishments in the life of a famous person, record historic moments in sports, create a video timeline of advancements in transportation, or document famous landmarks across America. Simply write a requirement sheet to let students know what information is required, and let their imaginations take over.

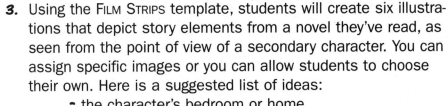

3. Using the FILM STRIPS template, students will create six illustrations that depict story elements from a novel they've read, as seen from the point of view of a secondary character. You can assign specific images or you can allow students to choose their own. Here is a suggested list of ideas:
   - the character's bedroom or home
   - the character's family and friends
   - other characters from the story
   - major events from the story
   - the main setting in the story
   - secondary settings in the story
   - the problem the character faces
   - the solution to this problem
   - the saddest, happiest, strangest, hardest event

4. Next, using the WRITING STRIPS template, have students write a descriptive paragraph to accompany each illustration. Their sentences should be written in the first person, as if the videographer were talking about the illustration as it was being filmed. Encourage students to be creative; the commentary should reflect the character's thoughts and feelings about the particular subject being filmed.

5. Hand out copies of the video camera templates on pages 129 and 130. Ask students to cut out and assemble the video cameras using the instructions on the templates. To make the frame sturdier, students can glue the templates to posterboard or oaktag.

6. Ask students to cut out their writing strips, put them in chronological order, and staple them to their video cameras where indicated.

7. Have students cut out the videotape frames and follow the directions on the template to thread the frames through the cameras. Have them tape craft sticks to the two ends of the videotape to prevent it from being pulled through the slots.

Teacher Tip

Kids love to see themselves on camera. Consider making a real videotaped movie of a novel your class read with the students acting out the characters in the story. The class can adapt the novel into a screenplay, pick locations, and decide on camera angles. Allow each student time to use the camera to shoot different scenes, and make sure everyone has a part. Host a premier party, and invite parents or other classes to view the movie.

Video Camera Cover

1. Glue the video camera cover to a sheet of posterboard and cut it out.
2. Write your name and the title of your report in the rectangle at the top of the video camera. Use decorative lettering.

Title:

Video Camera Interior

1. Glue the video camera interior to a sheet of posterboard and cut it out.
2. Tape the left edge of the cover to the left edge of the interior so it opens like a book.

Slot B

Cut slots A and B. Thread your film through slot A from behind and through slot B so only one frame can be seen at a time. Then tape each end tab around a craft stick to prevent it from being pulled through.

Slot A

Place writing strips here.

Put your writing strips in order and staple the left edges so they cover these instructions.

Film Strips

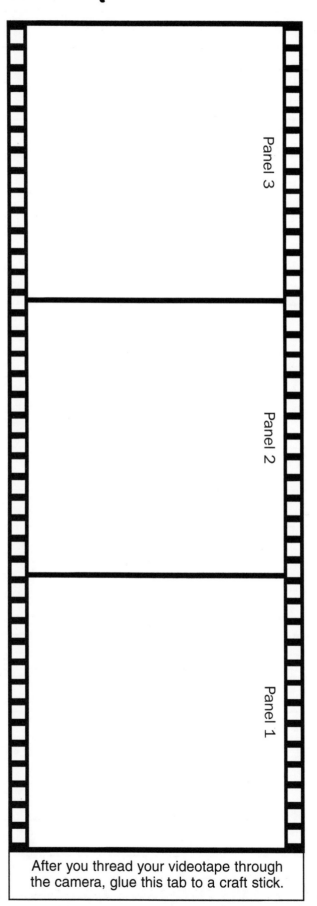

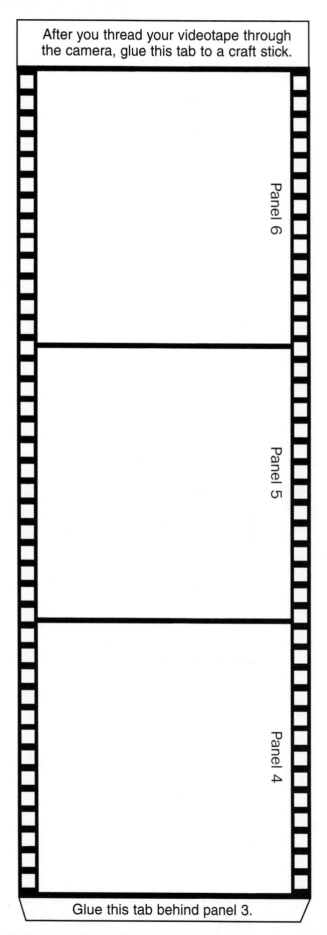

After you thread your videotape through the camera, glue this tab to a craft stick.

Panel 3

Panel 2

Panel 1

After you thread your videotape through the camera, glue this tab to a craft stick.

Panel 6

Panel 5

Panel 4

Glue this tab behind panel 3.

Writing Strips

Panel #   :

Panel #   :

Panel #   :

Panel #   :

An Explosive Situation

Materials

- 8¹/₂- by 11-inch sheets of copier paper
- 9- by 12-inch sheets of construction paper
- glue sticks
- scissors
- colored markers and pencils

Purpose

Students will identify and write about the conflict in a novel or story they've read.

Directions

1. Give each student a sheet of copier paper.

2. Direct students to fold the top right corner of the paper down diagonally to the left so that the top edge aligns with the left edge.

3. Have students cut off the bottom strip, leaving an 8¹/₂-inch square.

4. Explain to students that many works of fiction have a major conflict at their center and how these explosive situations give the stories their tension and keep the reader reading. Ask students to write two paragraphs on their sheet of paper— one that describes the situation before the conflict arises and another that describes how the conflict disrupts the relative calm that preceded it.

5. Ask students to fold the top left corner down diagonally so that the top edge of the paper aligns with the right edge, and then crease the fold. You should now have an X-shaped fold in the paper when it is open.

Teacher Tip

Discuss the four basic types of conflict that are found in literature— man vs. man, man vs. nature, man vs. society, and man vs. himself. Ask students to identify examples of conflict in movies they've seen or books they've read. Ask them to describe real-life examples they've seen in the news.

6. Instruct students to fold the top edge of the paper backward so it meets the bottom edge of the paper, with the writing on the outside. When opened the paper will have a horizontal crease.

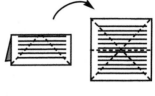

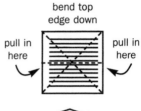

bend top edge down

pull in here

pull in here

7. Have students fold the top edge of the paper down to meet the bottom edge again (with the writing on the inside this time), pulling the two side edges into the center, forming a triangle. (The writing should be on the inside of this mechanism.)

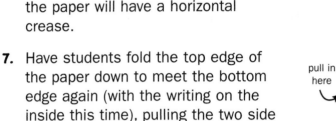

8. Ask students to fold the top triangle's right corner to the center of the baseline.

9. They should also do this with the left corner.

10. Then have them turn the triangle over and repeat.

11. Instruct students to reopen the four flaps they just created (as shown at right). Then have them push in the crease on the outer edge of each flap to create the "explosion" mechanism.

four flaps opened

push them into center

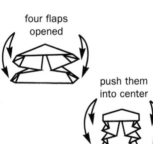

12. Then give each student a sheet of construction paper and ask them to fold it in half. This forms the cover for their card.

13. Ask students to glue the bottom side of the explosion into the card so that the point of the triangle touches the fold.

14. Finally, students can put glue on the top side of the explosion and close the card so it adheres. When the card is opened the the paper will burst open to reveal the writing.

15. Ask students to design a cover and title for the explosion card.

Caution: Hazard Ahead!

Materials

- 12- by 18-inch sheets of white construction paper
- colored markers and pencils

Purpose

Students will demonstrate a knowledge of the concept of problem and solution in a literary text.

Directions

1. Tell students to keep a list of problems and obstacles that the protagonist of a novel they're reading faces over the course of the story. They should conclude this list with the solution, goal, or accomplishment that ends the story.

2. Provide each student with a 12- by 18-inch sheet of white construction paper. Have students design a road that has a beginning and end. It can be a winding country road, a busy main street, a superhighway, a mountain trail, or a design of their choice. Encourage them to create a road that is representative of the novel they completed.

3. Have students design a "stop" along the road for each obstacle on their list. The stops can be traffic lights, stop signs, yield signs, broken bridges, exit ramps, detours, toll booths, washed-out roads, cattle crossings, nails, cliffs, and

Teacher Tip

Advise students to use pencil when designing their road in case they have to make changes. They can trace over the pencil with a black marker and then erase any stray pencil lines. This will give the maps a crisp, clean look, and it will teach students that presentation—as well as content—is an important part of their finished work.

other hazards. Make sure students label each stop with an obstacle from their list. The obstacles should be added to the road map in sequential order, starting with the first obstacle the protagonist faces and ending with the solution or goal achieved in the book.

4. Beneath each obstacle, ask students to write two complete sentences that describe important or interesting information about the event.

5. After students have designed their road maps and their stops, have them fill up any empty space with details that might be seen in the story's setting. For example, if the setting is rural, the student could include trees, barns, fields, and animals.

6. Next, have students fold their road map as shown below and use decorative lettering to write a map title on the small square panel at the front.

7. Finally, have students lift the title panels to reveal a long blank vertical panel. On this panel, have students write two complete paragraphs describing how the protagonist was affected or changed by the journey taken and the obstacles he or she faced.

1. Fold the map in half so that the illustration is on the outside.

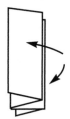

2. Fold the top and bottom panels back toward the first fold.

3. Fold the top half of the map down.

This Book Rocks!

The Tale of Despereaux
by: Kate DiCamillo

Materials

- 8½- by 11-inch sheets of white card stock
- compass
- scissors
- colored markers and pencils

Purpose

Students will describe things they liked and disliked about a book they've read.

Directions

1. Give students a sheet of white card stock and ask them to use a compass to draw an 8-inch circle on it.

2. Tell them to cut out the circle and fold it in half. When they tap the "rocker" it will move back and forth.

3. On one half of the outer side of the rocker, have students use decorative lettering to write the title of a book they are reviewing, the author's name, and their own name.

4. On the other half, have students draw a picture of an important scene from the book.

5. On the inside of the rocker, ask students to write a review of the book.

6. Line up the rockers on a shelf or counter. Add a banner that reads, THIS BOOK ROCKS!

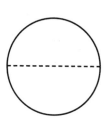

Criss Cross
by Lynne Rae
Perkins

Teacher Tip

Encourage students to think about adding details to or making simple cuts in the folded circle to create interesting shapes and animals that relate to the book they're reviewing.

Story Pyramids: Part 1

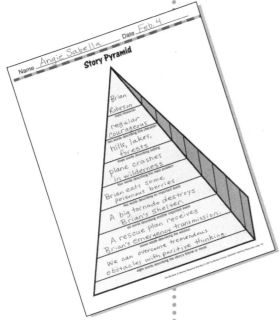

Materials

- STORY PYRAMID graphic organizer (page 139)

Purpose

Students will identify basic story elements in a book they've read.

Directions

1. Pass out copies of the STORY PYRAMID graphic organizer to the class.

2. Ask students to fill in the information on each level of the pyramid using the required number of words (no more, no less).

3. After students have completed their pyramids, ask volunteers to read theirs out loud, to share how they creatively filled in each of the levels.

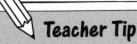

Teacher Tip

Adjust the directions on this graphic organizer to focus on specific story elements or concepts, such as minor characters, mood and atmosphere, and genre. Limiting the number of words students can use in their responses requires them to think creatively and concisely.

Name _____ Date _____

Story Pyramid

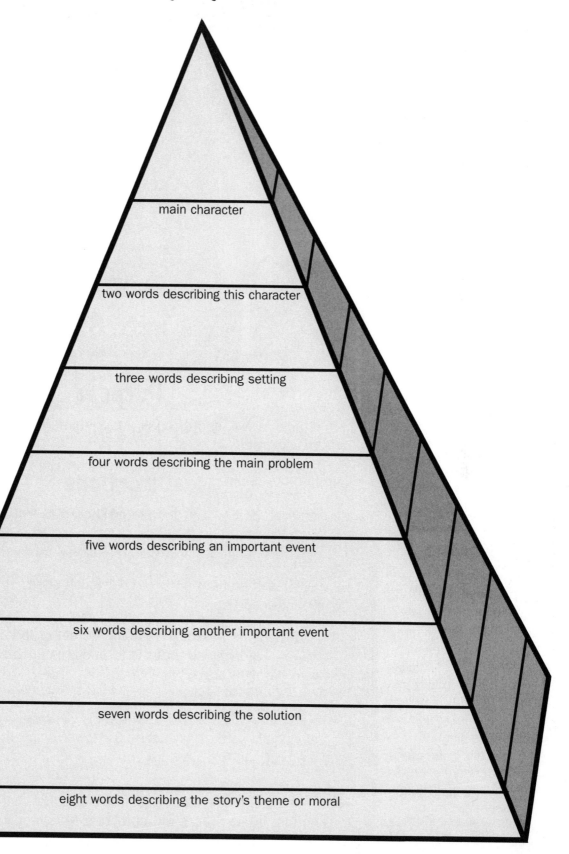

main character

two words describing this character

three words describing setting

four words describing the main problem

five words describing an important event

six words describing another important event

seven words describing the solution

eight words describing the story's theme or moral

Story Elements

Story Pyramids: Part 2

Materials

- 8 ¹/₂- by 14-inch sheets of white construction paper
- colored construction paper
- colored markers and pencils
- scissors
- glue sticks
- various craft materials

Purpose

Students will identify basic story elements in a book they've read.

Directions

1. After students have completed the STORY PYRAMID graphic organizer from page 139, ask them to focus on one of their answers to create a three-dimensional triorama pyramid.

2. Give each student an 8¹/₂- by 14-inch sheet of white construction paper.

3. Ask students to fold the top left corner of the paper diagonally so that the top edge is flush with the right edge.

4. Next have students fold the top right corner diagonally so that it touches the lower point of the previous fold.

5. Then have them fold the rectangular panel at the bottom up so that a horizontal crease is made.

Cross-Curriculum

Have students create triorama pyramids that focus on the lives of ancient Egyptians, Incas, or Mayans—societies that created pyramids. Trioramas could feature scenes dealing with their architecture, crafts, society, customs, rituals, technology, agriculture, language, and so on.

6. Have students open up the paper to reveal four triangular quadrants and a flap. Have them cut the diagonal crease between quadrants 1 and 4 up to the center point of the quadrants.

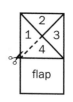

7. Tell students to think about the story element for which they are going to create a scene. Have them draw the background of this scene across quadrants 2 and 3. For example, if the scene takes place indoors, students might draw a background with wallpaper, paintings, and furniture. An outdoor scene might include a horizon with mountains.

background

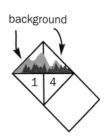

8. Have students draw the ground area for the scene on quadrant 1. For example, the ground for an indoor scene might include floorboards and a rug. An outdoor scene might feature grass or a pond.

ground

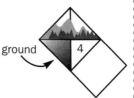

9. After students finish drawing the background and ground, show them how to pull point A over to point B. (Panel 1 will sit on top of panel 4.) This will cause the triorama to pop up into a triangular form. Tell students to glue the the bottom of panel 1 to the top of panel 4.

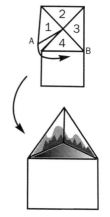

10. Encourage students to use construction paper, string, cotton, markers, craft sticks, and other craft materials to make the scene look as three-dimensional as possible. Suggest that they add a title banner across the top of the scene.

On this lower flap, students can write a paragraph about the story element shown on the triorama.

11. Tell students to use a ruler to lightly draw pencil lines on the bottom flap and write a complete, detailed paragraph describing the story element that is featured on the triorama pyramid. Remind them to erase the pencils lines after writing the paragraph.

Teacher Tip

Consider having students work in groups of four, with each member responsible for creating a triorama of a different story element. The four scenes can be glued back to back to form a four-sided pyramid display. The pyramids can be displayed on a table or countertop. Or each student can create two trioramas that can be glued side by side, to form a half-pyramid. These can be stapled to a bulletin board to create a display that really stands out!

Postcard Accordion Cases

Materials

- 12- by 18-inch sheets of construction paper
- 8½- by 11-inch sheets of white card stock
- rulers
- scissors
- glue sticks
- tape
- colored markers and pencils

Purpose

Students will identify and describe the significance different settings play in a novel they've recently read.

Directions

1. Give each student a sheet of construction paper and a sheet of card stock. Ask students to place the construction paper in front of them horizontally and fold up the bottom 4 inches, creating a long pocket.

2. Have students tape the two ends of the pocket closed.

3. Next, instruct them to fold the sheet in half so that the pocket is on the outside.

4. Then have them fold the two sides in half so that the pocket is on the inside of the accordion case.

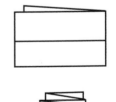

tape   tape

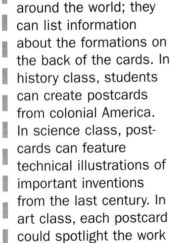

Cross-Curriculum

In geography class, students can design "fact files" that feature major land formations around the world; they can list information about the formations on the back of the cards. In history class, students can create postcards from colonial America. In science class, post-cards can feature technical illustrations of important inventions from the last century. In art class, each postcard could spotlight the work of a famous artist.

5. Have students cut off the top 2 inches of the accordion case.

6. Next, have students cut the sheet of card stock in half, vertically and horizontally, to make four postcards.

7. On each postcard, have students draw a picture of an important setting or location featured in a novel they've recently read. On the back of each card, encourage students to write a complete, detailed paragraph that describes the setting's significance in the story. Or you could have students write the postcards as if they were written by a character in the novel. Encourage students to design a stamp that is reflective of the setting.

8. When students have finished the four postcards, ask them to put each card into one of the pockets of the accordion case.

9. Invite students to design a cover for their case and give it a title that is related to the novel they read, such as POSTCARDS FROM THE ISLAND OF THE BLUE DOLPHIN.

Teacher Tip

For a more intensive, long-term project, students can create longer accordion cases by taping the last panel of one case to the first panel of another case. This could even be done as a whole-class project. Imagine a 50-panel accordion case that features a postcard from each state!

Travel Brochures

Materials

- 9- by 12-inch sheets of white construction paper
- rulers
- colored markers and pencils
- scissors

Purpose

Students will identify and describe a nonfictional setting from an informational text they have read.

Directions

1. Have students fold a sheet of white construction paper into thirds. The left panel should overlap the right panel. (The front cover will be called "panel 1;" the top of the right panel will be called "panel 2;" and the three interior panels will be called "panels 3, 4, and 5.")

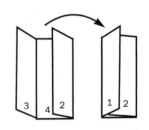

2. Tell students panel 1 should include a title, the name of the setting, and a slogan that would entice people to visit the place. At the top of the panel, have students draw an identifiable landmark or landform from the setting. The uppermost point of this illustration should be about 1½ to 2 inches from the top of the panel. After drawing and coloring the cover, students should cut away the excess paper above the top of the illustration.

Cut away gray area.

Visit
*Memphis,
Tennessee*
**Home
of the
Blues!**

Teacher Tip

Write to your state's department of tourism or visit a welcome center and request an assortment of travel brochures for your students to use as a model. You can also visit a local AAA (American Automobile Association) office and ask if it would supply pamphlets about the states for the class reference library.

3. On panel 2 students should draw a picture of a famous person from that setting so that his or her head and torso are at the right edge of panel 2. They should cut away the excess paper at the top left of the torso, cutting around the head as well. Below the figure, have students write the person's name and a paragraph describing him or her.

Cut away gray area.

ELVIS!

3   2

4. Panel 3 has been cut in the shape of the landform or landmark that is on the cover. Students should hold panel 3 up to a classroom window and trace the image from panel 1 and then color it. Below this drawing, students should write a paragraph describing this important sight.

5. Tell students to draw a skyline or horizon line of the setting across the top of panel 4. The skyline should feature important buildings, landmarks, or landforms. Have students cut away the excess paper from above this silhouette. Underneath this illustration have them write a paragraph describing the setting. (See the photo below.)

6. Panel 5 is on the back of the one featuring the famous person. On this panel, students should list some interesting facts about the setting. Or, if the setting is used in a fiction book they read, students can write a paragraph discussing the importance of the setting in the story, why the author chose to set the story in this particular setting, or how the story would have changed had the setting been different.

Teacher Tip

Display the travel guides by stapling the interior middle panel to a bulletin board. The left and right panels can then be opened by anyone interested in learning more about the setting described in the brochure.

Beginning, Middle, and End

CD Covers

1. I Told You It Was Round!
2. Help Me, Isabella
3. This Ain't the West Indies
4. In Fourteen Ninety-Two
5. They Call Me Cristobal
6. Land Ho!
7. San Salvador, Holy Savior
8. Dance Like an Arawak
9. Oh Six and Penniless
10. Amerigo? What About Me?

Materials

- sheets of light-colored construction paper
- rulers
- scissors
- glue sticks
- colored markers and pencils

Purpose

Students will create song titles and lyrics that express the main ideas of a novel's plot.

Directions

1. Give each student a sheet of light-colored construction paper and ask them to cut a strip that measures 5 by 10 inches.

2. Ask them to fold this strip in half so the front measures 5 inches square.

3. Tell students they will be creating a CD cover, a list of songs, and a song related to a novel they've recently read.

4. On the front cover, students should use construction paper and colored markers or pencils to create a cover design and title for the CD.

5. On the back cover, students should create a list of ten song titles that relate to the content of the novel they've read.

6. Ask students to open up the CD cover and write the lyrics for a song that conveys the main idea of the beginning, middle, and end of the novel. Have students set the lyrics to the melody of a popular song.

7. When they are finished, encourage volunteers to sing their songs for the class.

Teacher Tip

To encourage shy students, group the class in twos or threes. Have each group write a song together. Each group member can write the lyrics in the CD cover that he or she designed. Then the groups can sing their songs together. Remember, there's safety in numbers!

ABC Stories

Materials

- writing paper
- colored markers and pencils

Purpose

Students will write sentences of varying lengths and complexity to convey their comprehension of a literary or informational text.

Directions

1. Ask students to use colored markers and pencils to design a sheet of stationery. The sheet should have a border of images related to a novel they've read.

2. Explain that good writers vary the lengths and types of sentences they use. This makes their writing more interesting and less monotonous.

3. Ask students to retell the story of the novel they read in twenty-six sentences. Each sentence should begin with a different letter of the alphabet, starting with A and ending with Z. This simple constraint will force the students to come up with creative solutions to retell the story, and it will make them examine sentence structure, length, transition words, and introductory phrases and clauses in unexpected ways.

Teacher Tip

Ask students to glue their finished stories to a sheet of colored construction paper to add a more finished look to these projects. The stories can then be hung on a bulletin board under a banner that reads, THE ABCs OF GOOD WRITING.

Biographies

Pop Stars

Materials

- empty two-liter soda bottles
- sandpaper
- paint
- construction paper
- craft materials
- glue
- colored markers and pencils
- writing paper
- scissors

Purpose

Students will turn old soda-pop bottles into a lineup of famous people whose lives they have studied.

Directions

1. Have students peel the label off an empty soda bottle.

2. Ask them to rub sandpaper on the surface of the bottle so that paint will adhere. Then have them paint the bottle to look like the famous person whose biography they read.

3. Encourage them to use construction paper and craft materials to add a hat, scarf, hair, buttons, arms, hands, or facial features.

4. Give students a sheet of writing paper, and have them write a few paragraphs about the person or create a timeline of his or her life that notes important events and achievements.

5. Have students cut a hole in the back of the bottle and insert their report.

6. Line up the pop bottles on a shelf or counter.

Teacher Tip

Encourage creative writing by having your students create a soda bottle superhero. Tell them to write a story that describes the origins of his or her superpower or that chronicles one of his or her adventures.

Comparative Timelines

Materials

- TIMELINE template (page 150)
- bulletin board paper
- colored markers and pencils
- tape

Purpose

Students will create a bulletin board that juxtaposes events from a historical novel with events that occurred in real life.

Directions

1. Cut a long sheet of bulletin board paper to the length of a bulletin board, and draw a horizontal line across the middle to create the timeline.

2. After reading a historical novel have the class brainstorm a list of events that happened in the novel. These events can be fictional or actual. Then have students brainstorm a second list of events that actually happened in the world at the time in which the novel was set. These events may or may not have been a part of the story's plot.

3. Divide the class in half, and give each student a copy of the TIMELINE template. Half the class will report on events from the novel. The other half will report on real-life events. Assign each student an event. Have them write the event's date on the top line of the template, draw a picture of it, and write a descriptive paragraph.

4. Tape the templates in chronological order on the timeline. Tape the real events above the line and the events from the novel below the line.

✳ Cross-Curriculum

Create timelines that trace the adventures and discoveries of famous explorers, major battles of the Civil War, important inventions, or the life of a well-known composer.

Name _____ Date _____

Timeline Template

_____
(Date of Event)

_____

_____

_____

_____

_____

_____

_____

_____

Tear-Art Book Covers

Materials

- examples of Impressionist paintings
- posterboard
- colored construction paper
- glue sticks

Purpose

As a culminating activity at the end of the school year, students will create posters of favorite books they've read throughout the year.

Directions

1. Show students examples of such Impressionist paintings as *Sunday Afternoon on the Island of La Grande Jatte* by Georges Seurat, *Mother About to Wash Her Sleepy Child* by Mary Cassatt, and *Water Lilies* by Claude Monet. Discuss how these paintings do not give every detail of the people and objects in them but convey their essence through color and shape.

2. Ask each student to choose a favorite book they've read in class or at home for which they'd like to create an impressionistic book cover.

3. Invite students to make a rough sketch on the posterboard where they want to place the major elements of their book cover.

4. Tell students to tear pieces of construction paper into the shapes they want for the poster. No scissors allowed! The torn edges of the paper will give the posters an impressionistic, free-form quality.

5. Have students glue the pieces in place, overlapping them for a subtle 3-D effect.

6. On the back of the posters, have students write a few paragraphs describing why they chose the book and what they liked most about it.

Cross-Curriculum

Encourage cooperation and teamwork by inviting your class to create a tear art mural of an animal habitat or of the four seasons. Lay a long sheet of bulletin board paper on the floor and have the class sit beside it to create the mural. Students will have to talk to the students on either side of them to coordinate a scene that flows. Hang the mural in the hallway for everyone to enjoy.

Book Reports

Newbery Medal Reports

Materials

- NEWBERY REPORT requirement sheet (page 154)
- NEWBERY REPORT templates (pages 155–157)
- colored markers and pencils
- scissors
- brass paper fasteners

Purpose

Students will demonstrate a knowledge of story structure, character development, setting, and other story elements as they create a report on an award-winning book.

Directions

1. Distribute one copy of the NEWBERY REPORT template 1 (using yellow paper makes the award look like a gold medal) and multiple copies of templates 2 and 3 to each student.

2. Invite your school librarian to come in and discuss the history of the Newbery Medal, its significance, and why it was named after John Newbery. Have the librarian bring in samples of Newbery winners and honor books.

3. Pass out a copy of the NEWBERY REPORT requirement sheet and review it with your students.

4. Ask students to choose a Newbery Medal winner or honor book to read.

5. Have students read their chosen book and use the templates to create their book report.

6. After students have finished the pages, have them cut out the shapes, punch holes in the asterisks (*), and fasten the pages together with two brass fasteners.

Teacher Tip

Since 1922, the Newbery Medal has been awarded each year to the author of an outstanding children's book. A list of Newbery winners can be found on page 153. You may want to copy and display this list to help students choose books for their reports. Students can also choose Newbery honor books if they prefer.

Newbery Medal Winners

2007
The Higher Power of Lucky
Susan Patron

2006
Criss Cross
Lynne Rae Perkins

2005
Kira-Kira
Cynthia Kadohata

2004
The Tale of Despereaux
Kate DiCamillo

2003
Crispin: The Cross of Lead
Avi

2002
A Single Shard
Linda Sue Park

2001
A Year Down Yonder
Richard Peck

2000
Bud, Not Buddy
Christopher Paul Curtis

1999
Holes
Louis Sachar

1998
Out of the Dust
Karen Hesse

1997
The View from Saturday
E. L. Konigsburg

1996
The Midwife's Apprentice
Karen Cushman

1995
Walk Two Moons
Sharon Creech

1994
The Giver
Lois Lowry

1993
Missing May
Cynthia Rylant

1992
Shiloh
Phyllis Reynolds Naylor

1991
Maniac Magee
Jerry Spinelli

1990
Number the Stars
Lois Lowry

1989
Joyful Noise: Poems for Two Voices
Paul Fleischman

1988
Lincoln: A Photobiography
Russell Freedman

1987
The Whipping Boy
Sid Fleischman

1986
Sarah, Plain and Tall
Patricia MacLachlan

1985
The Hero and the Crown
Robin McKinley

1984
Dear Mr. Henshaw
Beverly Cleary

1983
Dicey's Song
Cynthia Voigt

1982
A Visit to William Blake's Inn
Nancy Willard

1981
Jacob Have I Loved
Katherine Paterson

1980
A Gathering of Days
Joan W. Blos

1979
The Westing Game
Ellen Raskin

1978
Bridge to Terabithia
Katherine Paterson

1977
Roll of Thunder, Hear My Cry
Mildred D. Taylor

1976
The Grey King
Susan Cooper

1975
M. C. Higgins, the Great
Virginia Hamilton

1974
The Slave Dancer
Paula Fox

1973
Julie of the Wolves
Jean Craighead George

1972
Mrs. Frisby and the Rats of NIMH
Robert C. O'Brien

1971
Summer of the Swans
Betsy Byars

1970
Sounder
William Armstrong

1969
The High King
Lloyd Alexander

1968
From the Mixed-Up Files of Mrs. Basil E. Frankweiler
E. L. Konigsburg

1967
Up a Road Slowly
Irene Hunt

1966
I, Juan de Pareja
Elizabeth Borton de Trevino

1965
Shadow of a Bull
Maia Wojciechowska

1964
It's Like This, Cat
Emily Neville

1963
A Wrinkle in Time
Madeleine L'Engle

1962
The Bronze Bow
Elizabeth G. Speare

1961
Island of the Blue Dolphins
Scott O'Dell

1960
Onion John
Joseph Krumgold

1959
The Witch of Blackbird Pond
Elizabeth G. Speare

1958
Rifles for Watie
Harold Keith

1957
Miracles on Maple Hill
Virginia Sorenson

1956
Carry On, Mr. Bowditch
Jean Lee Latham

1955
The Wheel on the School
Meindert DeJong

1954
. . . And Now Miguel Joseph Krumgold

1953
Secret of the Andes
Ann Nolan Clark

1952
Ginger Pye
Eleanor Estes

1951
Amos Fortune, Free Man
Elizabeth Yates

1950
The Door in the Wall
Marguerite de Angeli

1949
King of the Wind
Marguerite Henry

1948
The Twenty-One Balloons
William Pène du Bois

1947
Miss Hickory
Carolyn S. Bailey

1946
Strawberry Girl
Lois Lenski

1945
Rabbit Hill
Robert Lawson

1944
Johnny Tremain
Esther Forbes

1943
Adam of the Road
Elizabeth J. Gray

1942
The Matchlock Gun
Walter Edmonds

1941
Call It Courage
Armstrong Sperry

1940
Daniel Boone
James Daugherty

1939
Thimble Summer
Elizabeth Enright

1938
The White Stag
Kate Seredy

1937
Roller Skates
Ruth Sawyer

1936
Caddie Woodlawn
Carol Ryrie Brink

1935
Dobry
Monica Shannon

1934
Invincible Louisa
Cornelia Meigs

1933
Young Fu of the Upper Yangtze
Elizabeth Lewis

1932
Waterless Mountain
Laura A. Armer

1931
The Cat Who Went to Heaven
Elizabeth Coatsworth

1930
Hitty, Her First Hundred Years
Rachel Field

1929
The Trumpeter of Krakow
Eric P. Kelly

1928
Gay Neck
Dhan Gopal Mukerji

1927
Smoky, the Cowhorse
Will James

1926
Shen of the Sea
Arthur B. Chrisman

1925
Tales from Silver Lands
Charles Finger

1924
The Dark Frigate
Charles Hawes

1923
The Voyages of Doctor Dolittle
Hugh Lofting

1922
The Story of Mankind
Hendrik van Loon

Newbery Report
Requirement Sheet

☐ **Cover**

Use template 1. In the center of the medal use decorative lettering to write the name of the book and the author's name. Also include your name at the bottom.

☐ **Summary**

Use template 2 and label it "Summary" at the top. Then write a summary of the book. Use additional templates if needed. Your summary should include a brief description of the following story elements—main characters, setting, major events, problem/solution, and conclusion.

☐ **Favorite Scene**

Use template 3 and label it "Favorite Scene." Draw a picture of your favorite scene. Write a sentence describing the scene below it.

☐ **Main Character**

Use template 2 and label it "Main Character." Write a paragraph describing the main character. Tell how he or she changed throughout the course of the story—physically, emotionally, intellectually, spiritually, morally, socially.

☐ **Important Scene**

Use template 3 and label it "Important Scene." Draw a picture of the main character in an important scene from the book. Write a sentence describing what is happening.

☐ **Main Problem**

Use template 2 and label it "Main Problem." Write a detailed paragraph about the main problem in the story. Write a second paragraph describing the solution.

☐ **Problem/Solution**

Use template 3. Draw a line down the middle, and label the left half "Problem" and the right half "Solution." Then draw a picture of the main problem and solution in the story. Write a simple sentence describing each illustration.

☐ **New Character**

Use template 3 and label it "Me As a New Character." Write a paragraph that answers the questions: If you yourself were a *new* character in the book, what would your role be? What would you have done in the story? Would your character change the outcome of the story? What would your relationship with other characters be? Would you be a main character or a secondary character?

☐ **Why This Book Is a Winner**

Use template 2 and label it "Why This Book Is a Winner." There must have been a good reason your book was a Newbery Medal winner or honor book. What was it about your book that made it so outstanding? Write a complete and thoughtful paragraph. Cite examples from the book to support your opinion.

☐ **Vocabulary**

Use template 2 and label it "Vocabulary." As you read your book, look up words whose meanings you don't know. List alphabetically ten words that were unfamiliar to you when you first read the book along with their definitions.

Newbery Report
Template 1

JOHN · NEWBERY · MEDAL

Book Report By:

Newbery Report
Template 2

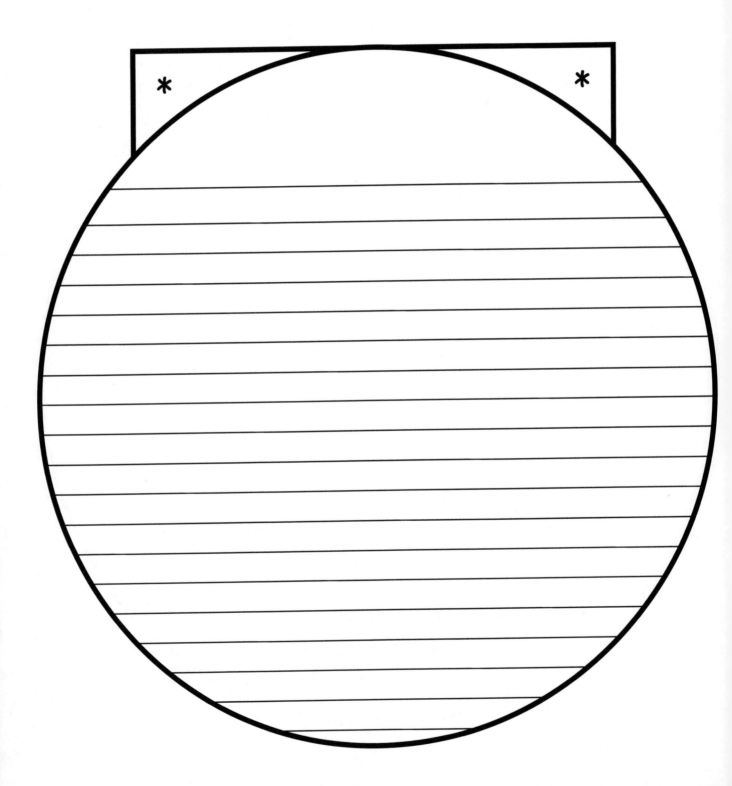

Newbery Report
Template 3

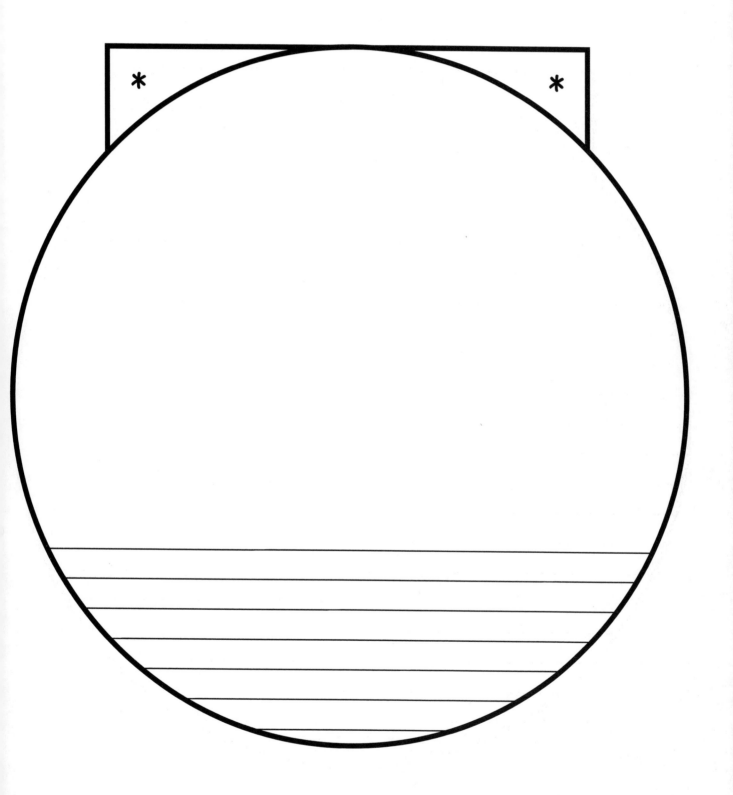

Book Reports

Tunnel Books

THE DIAMONDBACK RATTLESNAKE

Materials

- 12- by 18-inch sheets of construction paper
- scissors
- rulers
- 5³/₄- by 8³/₄-inch pieces of oaktag or white card stock
- colored markers and pencils
- glue sticks

Purpose

Students will demonstrate a knowledge of story structure, character development, setting, and other story elements as they create an expandable 3-D report for a book they've read.

Directions

1. Give each student an 12- by 18-inch sheet of construction paper and have them cut it in half vertically, giving them two 6- by 18-inch strips.

2. Have students lay a strip in front of them horizontally and draw a vertical line 1 inch from the right edge. Have them draw eight more lines, each 1 inch to the left of the previous line. The strip should now have nine vertical lines.

3. Instruct students to fan-fold the strip along each of the lines, as shown at right.

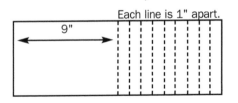

Each line is 1" apart.

9"

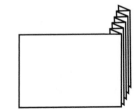

Teacher Tip

Lead a genre study and ask each student to create a diorama scene from a book of a particular genre. Cover panels can include a list of nouns found in the setting, a paragraph describing how the story would change if it were placed in a different setting, a synopsis of the plot, an analysis of why this book belongs to this particular genre, or a description of the student's favorite scene. Line up the diorama books on a shelf or countertop for everyone to enjoy.

4. Have students repeat steps 2 and 3 with the second strip. These two strips will act as the frame for the diorama book. The unfolded halves of the sheets will serve as the covers.

5. Give students nine $5^3/_4$- by $8^3/_4$-inch pieces of oaktag or white card stock.

6. Ask students to sketch on a sheet of scratch paper an important scene from a novel they've read. This scene should include foreground, midground, and background objects.

7. Have students use a ruler to draw a border around the perimeter of four pieces of oaktag; the bottom border should be 1 inch, and the three others should be $^1/_2$ inch.

8. On the first piece of oaktag, have students draw some foreground objects from the scene; the items should touch the border (such as the rattlesnake in the example at right). Have students cut away the blank area (as shown in gray at right).

9. On the second piece of oaktag, have students draw some objects or people that appear just behind the foreground objects (such as the dunes and the large cactus in the example). To determine the placement of these objects, students 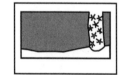 should place the second piece of oaktag behind the "window" they cut in the first piece and mark the objects' placement. After students draw the objects, have them cut away the blank area (as shown in gray at right).

10. On the third sheet of oaktag, have students draw some objects or people that appear a little further back in the scene (such as the dunes and the two cacti in the example). To determine the placement of these objects, 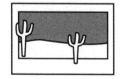 students should place the third piece of oaktag behind the windows they cut in the first and second pieces. After students draw the objects, have them cut away the blank area.

11. The fourth piece of oaktag shows objects that appear just in front of the background (such as the hills in the example). After students draw the objects, have them cut away the blank area.

Cross-Curriculum

Let history come alive with three-dimensional displays of important events from earlier eras. Dinosaurs can roam the planet once again, pyramids can be built in ancient Egypt, or the Wright brothers can fly at Kittyhawk.

Book Talk

"I've traveled the world twice over,
Met the famous; saints and sinners,
Poets and artists, kings and queens,
Old stars and hopeful beginners,
I've been where no-one's been before,
Learned secrets from writers and cooks
All with one library ticket
To the wonderful world of books."
—Author Unknown

12. On a full piece of oaktag have students illustrate the background objects (such as the sun and sky in the example).

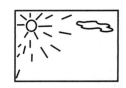

13. Show students how to take the two pieces of construction paper with the accordion folds and place the cover of the left side of the frame over the cover of the right side of the frame (as shown at right). The front cover opens to the left. The second cover opens to the right.

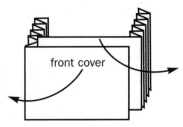

14. Instruct students to put glue on the back of the right and left sides of the background picture and glue it to the back tabs on the two frames.

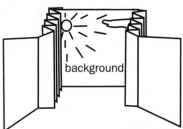

15. The fourth piece of oaktag can be glued to the fourth tabs of the frame, the third piece to the third tabs, the second piece to the second tabs, and the first piece to the front tabs just behind the two covers. The diorama will have a true sense of perspective when the fan-fold is opened.

16. On the remaining four pieces of oaktag students can write a book report, draw illustrations, provide character sketches, create a graphic organizer, list vocabulary words, or create a cover illustration for the diorama book; you can decide on the requirements. Have students glue these panels onto the front and back of the two covers. (The oaktag will provide support, making the book more durable.)

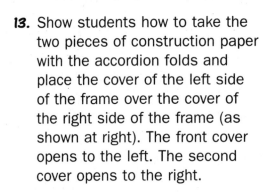